Centering Prayer

Healing Our God Wound

Kevin Sharpe

Imagine That! Publishing Group

ISBN: 978-1-959970-04-0

Do not be afraid, for I am with you.

Isaiah 41:10

CONTENTS

PREFACE

The subtitle of this book, *Healing Our God Wound*, hits close to home for me. Like many, I am someone who was formed, from early in life, by dint of a God wound. I have also suffered through a religion wound, or to be more specific, a Christianity wound. Today, I stand on the other side, healed of those wounds, thanks in large part to centering prayer. In truth, a small constellation of "points of light" lives in that phrase *centering prayer*, and I don't want to come across as reductionist when I use it in a sort of shorthand fashion. Framing the conversation with that understanding, centering prayer as a practice has been and remains instrumental for many as they discover a healthy relationship with God.

Because of my own journey through a terrain disfigured by religion and God wounds and after having gained lived experience of how radically better life can be on the other side of these wounds, I started to have conversations with others, and became witness to story after story of similar wounding expressed with both passion and vulnerability. Since centering prayer played such an integral role in my own healing, it began to feel big and quite important to find a way to hold up, put forth, and explore centering prayer as a means to heal these wounds. In large part, that is the reason this book exists.

To be fully transparent, this particular book is the first in a trilogy of titles that together focus on this phenomenon of healing back into God, this healing into a mature and healthy relationship with the Divine. In the pages of this book, we explore the *praxis* or the essential practice of this process known as centering prayer.

This book is a primer on centering prayer. It's not so much a "how to" book but more of an approach to centering prayer as a path that leads to the restoration and deepening of our subjective and experiential relationship with God. This unfolding of relationship implies, at its very foundation, a healing. It's the door through which anyone with wounds must walk.

Kevin Sharpe
From the Outskirts of Eden
September 01, 2024

INTRODUCTION

It's an unsteady and challenging landscape here along this path eastward. For each step I physically take, I take two in my mind. It makes the journey twice as long and often twice as arduous. Honestly, I don't know where this path leads. Not many I encounter along the way do. Sometimes when I take a moment to rest my feet, a thought lodges in my mind and tugs at my heart. It's something like a memory of some home I can't quite recall yet somehow long for. The memory calls out for me to turn and look westward into the distance, toward the setting sun and the land of my heart, toward the land of Eden and the home I'm walking away from, knowing that it becomes more of a distant and fading memory with each step into this world where I now find myself, into this land east of Eden.

It's with this sobering and perhaps poignant image along with any feelings it evokes that we begin this book on centering prayer.

What to do with this image, this metaphor for the life we live on some level? In brief, the answer lives in the following bold and hopeful statement.

> *Centering prayer is a way for us to return to the Eden of our heart, which is ultimately an intimate, vulnerable, and deep relationship with God.*

This statement encourages and motivates us to discover and engage centering prayer, bringing sure resolution to the opening image however it may have landed in body and mind as we read and imagined it.

It's a good place to start a book like this.

Where We Are

The opening image calls to us from that time after God has cast humanity out of Eden, into a land to the east. (If you're triggered by the image of "God casting out," notice if you can be present to that while you continue reading.) The image serves, in a certain way, to validate our experience here, today, in this land east of Eden. The legacy we have inherited from that pivotal moment of exile and that has formed our lives is a legacy of having been not just cast out but cast to the margins, out of conscious relationship with God and into that condition most easily characterized by all its harshness.

Some of us are more aware than others of the pain and suffering and disarray that this causes. Regardless of the level of our awareness, it is nonetheless on the margins that we do find ourselves living, making our lives into something that gets us simply (and often with trepidation) from one moment to the next. Yet, if we're honest, we sense deep within ourselves, on a cellular level, that this place we live, this life we've created east of Eden, is missing something. It's missing *home*. And the integral ingredient that makes Eden, Eden and that makes *home*, *home* is God—more specifically our intimate, conscious, and life-giving relationship with God.

Those of us who are waking up and encountering the unsettling awareness that we have indeed been cast to the margins come to realize that we are wounded rather profoundly. This results in our living broken lives. Truthfully, on some level, we are all broken; and on some level, we are all seeking the healing of that brokenness—a restoration and deepening of relationship with God. We are all seeking this return to Eden, where we walk in the gentle evening breeze with God. That is the life we yearn for. That is the life we seek.

Enter Centering Prayer

Centering prayer gives us opportunity to be with the God of and in our hearts in a very intimate way. Reflect a moment on that statement. Let its profundity settle into your body, into your mind, and into your heart.

Through this intimate and personal form of prayer, we experience a depth of encounter that harmonizes the apparent incongruity presented to us in Genesis: the God who is all love has cast us out of Eden. Bypassing this foundational incongruity creates such a profound dissonance within the core of our being that it reverberates out into our world, leaving a dull hum of discord in its wake that infects and inflicts every relationship in life.

This book focuses on how to engage centering prayer as a full praxis or practice to support restoring and deepening our subjective relationship with God. It accomplishes this using a four-fold approach:

1. Exposing and unpacking a little-known set of centering prayer instructions found in Psalm 62,

2. Offering questions for reflection and exploration based on each reader's unique life experiences,

3. Working with imagination-based exercises to move concepts from the page and the mind into the body,

4. Providing nuanced centering prayer practices based on each particular instruction from Psalm 62.

This approach to centering prayer consciously tries to find novel language to describe and reframe important Christian concepts, which may have been transmitted to us encrusted with a legacy of fear and control and judgment. The intention behind reframing these concepts is to help make them come alive and support us as well as enrich our centering prayer experiences, leading to a deeper relationship with God.

We begin with getting clear about what exactly centering prayer is. In the process, we establish some guide rails to use for setting out on the path of this form of Christian prayer.

Then we introduce Psalm 62 as a type of map of the landscape or a template of the dynamics of centering prayer, preparing us for the journey we may encounter during a typical centering prayer experience.

Next, we explore Psalm 62 as a unique text of instructions that offers insight into centering prayer's depth, and how it both affects and effects subjective relationship with God and ourselves. For those new to centering prayer, this section will be immensely supportive. For those who already have a centering prayer praxis, this section will offer glimpses that both validate and provide insight into personal experiences with God born out of centering prayer.

Whether you're pursuing centering prayer on your own, with a spiritual director, or as part of a centering prayer group, you'll discover in the pages of this book a good spiritual companion and guide to accompany you on this life-changing journey into the dynamic landscape of centering prayer.

1

PRAXIS

I MAKE TIME TO be alone with Christ, come what may.

There is an early morning chill in the darkness as I light the single candle that stands on my home altar. The candlelight bathes the room in a soft warm glow. I take a moment to become present to the chill in the air, the soft warm glow, and the steadily burning candle flame. Then I take my seat.

I sit on a thin cotton mat that covers the hardwood floor in front of the altar. My legs are crossed; my hands are on my knees; my back is straight. This is how I sit.

I breathe deeply and gently through my nose as I follow a few breaths into and out of my body. Then I silently and slowly say to myself: "For God alone, my soul in silence waits."

Twenty minutes pass, and I bring my awareness back to my breath as I open my eyes. I take a moment to place the soles of my bare feet onto the floor as I bring my legs together and hug them into my chest. A moment more and I slowly stand.

Praxis is a word that is gaining more traction beyond contemplative circles. It's a good word to understand. It comes to us from Greek and means *a doing*. More precisely, *praxis* is most akin to a practice, something done regularly and over an extended period of time. Some good examples of *praxis* include activities like meditation, *lectio divina*, prayer, and of course, centering prayer.

Often in this book, the word *praxis* is used instead of the word *practice*. The reason is simple and important. Using the word *practice* may lure us (at least on a subtle level) into thinking that our *practice* takes practice and is meant to improve over time. This kind of thinking can even lead us to giving up on centering prayer. With that in mind, it's helpful to remember that the goal of any contemplative praxis is not for it to improve over time. Rather, the goal of our praxis is to let it transform us over time.

How that transformation looks will vary from person to person. It can deepen our faith. It can support us on a journey toward healing. It can certainly nourish our souls as we move deeply into conscious relationship with God.

The description at the start of this chapter reveals a typical centering prayer experience as viewed from the outside and brings to light two facts worth keeping in mind. The first is the importance the role of place plays in centering prayer. It's good to find a quiet place and sit either on the floor or in a chair. It can be supportive if this place has a sense or feeling of sacredness, some place that is somewhat set apart.

The second fact to notice is that there is an implied commitment to centering prayer as a praxis. In other words, it's not typically an activity done every now and then. Rather, to have centering prayer serve us most effectively in healing and deepening our relationship with God, we need to make a commitment to it. To that end, two key aspects become essential.

The first aspect is frequency. In particular, how often will we not just commit to engaging our chosen praxis, but how often can we realistically engage it? For example, a person may have the best of intentions of sitting in centering prayer for 20 minutes twice daily. However, is that frequency realistic given all the other commitments in their life? If it isn't realistic, then that person would do well to choose something more realistic, perhaps once per day for 20 minutes. For very busy folks, this choice is more manageable and is also something that they can successfully commit to. It's through regularly showing up for centering prayer that familiarity with the technique develops and the fruits of centering prayer mature.

The second aspect is long-term commitment. Quite simply, this means that we keep showing up for our praxis, day in and day out. When life is joyful, we show up. When life is challenging, we show up. When life is overwhelming, we show up. Ironically, sometimes the most resistance we will find to showing up for our praxis is when life is joyful and going along quite smoothly. Humanity, in general, tends to look to God when things are difficult. We tend to disregard God when things are going well. The key (and the challenge) is to keep God in our lives during both the joy and the suffering.

It's good to take a moment to become aware of some emotional games we may play with ourselves around our showing up and not showing up for centering prayer. Three of these "mind trips" include guilt, shame, and frustration.

Guilt

Guilt is a type of psychological discomfort that we experience by missing a mark that we have agreed to. It's a feeling that penetrates a particular moment. For example, we commit to one period of centering prayer each day. After four days, we notice that we've missed two of the periods and, as such, have been missing our mark. Now, each time we miss it, we feel guilt.

As the trend continues, our guilt builds. We eventually react and drop centering prayer to dissipate the uncomfortable feelings that accompany the guilt. We then legitimize our reaction in order to alleviate having to face any ensuing guilt due to giving up our praxis. That legitimization may be as simple as telling ourselves that we were already overcommitted and responsible for too long of a list of obligations.

Shame

Shame is a feeling that can often become conflated with guilt. However, a difference between the two exists. Whereas guilt is usually expressed as a targeted feeling such as *I feel guilt because...*, shame is a smoldering fire of malaise which blazes up, at times scorching new areas of a person's being. Shame is usually expressed through self-identification with an offending quality. A few examples of how it may be expressed include *I am bad* or *I am selfish* or *I am not worthy of love*. Essentially, shame is internalized and becomes intrinsic.

While guilt can have a short-term effect, causing us to react to a particular event or experience, the pain from shame can reach into the distant future and potentially have long-term influence over how we move through our entire life.

How might shame show up in relation to a centering prayer praxis? For a person with a God wound, shame may already be influencing one's life choices. In other words, such a person may start to explore centering prayer while already self-identifying as too unworthy or too broken or too evil for God. Then when actions don't meet expectations, the shame gets triggered. Instead of taking time to assess and regroup to discover the cause of the centering prayer "hiccup," the triggered person quickly finds a way out of the experience and any future triggers through tactics like self-fulfilling prophecies (i.e., *I knew I was too broken for God*), which unfortunately reinforces the shame while dismissing centering prayer as a praxis and as a way out of the shame.

Frustration

On the surface, frustration may seem to exist in a different and less-intense category than guilt or shame. The important consideration here is to realize that frustration can wield an immense amount of power over our decisions, and all of us are susceptible to it. As it relates to centering prayer, feelings of frustration may lead one to discount the value of centering prayer.

As an example, let's say we start a new praxis of centering prayer only to find it challenging. Perhaps we find it difficult to silence our internal chatter, struggle to remain present for 20 minutes. It's certainly understandable that this scenario could lead to frustration with the praxis itself or with ourselves for not being able to "do" it. To bypass the frustration, we look for a way to escape its apparent cause: our commitment to centering prayer. Frustration offers us thoughts to legitimize our escape. For example, centering prayer is simply not for me. It's an easy out. It's rational, and it even may feel true, in the moment. It's something we can tell ourselves and others, and then move on.

Addressing the Three Big Emotional Games

Even for longtime practitioners of centering prayer, the praxis can be challenging at times, and any or all of the big three energetics or forces described above may show up. The key to maintaining a centering prayer praxis is to notice the emotional games in play and to keep showing up in spite of them.

Step one is essentially to become aware of the feeling (guilt, shame, frustration) when it arises. If it arises during centering prayer, do nothing with the feeling. Just let it be. In other words, don't act or react in its wake. Given time, and if we do not spin up stories about it, the feeling will run its course.

If we notice one of these feelings arising after our praxis period, then we would do well to notice if we start to move in the direction of discounting the value of centering prayer or even rationalizing that it isn't for us because of x or y or z. Both of these tactics are paths that may lead to bowing out of our commitment.

Instead of dropping our praxis, what would it be like to explore other potential psychological energetics (i.e., perfectionism, control, fear) that may be at play underneath or in league with these primary energetics of guilt, shame, and frustration. Then, once identified, we may want to take time to reflect on how they're showing up in other areas of our life. Such an exploration could be both eye opening and worthwhile.

While opting out of centering prayer is always a possibility, staying with the praxis will actually move us in the direction of healing these controlling energetics.

Contextualizing Commitment

For our spiritual praxis to be supportive, we know we need to commit to doing it both regularly and over a long period of time. Knowing about some of the energetics that can get in the way of our centering prayer praxis as we start out can help us hone the skill of internal awareness and give us insight into our own psyche. At the end of the day, however, commitment is a choice.

The first sentence of this chapter speaks to the importance of the role of prioritization in relation to choice. Let's take another look at that first sentence: *I make time to be with Christ, come what may.* It points to centering prayer being not just high on the list of priorities, but actually holding the first position on that list.

It's important to remember that if we do not consciously choose for our centering prayer praxis each day, then it will become easier to choose for something else. It's a slippery slope that starts innocently enough, but quickly has us falling prey to the busyness of life and potentially to one of the energetics mentioned above. If this happens, the likelihood of dropping centering prayer entirely may not be far behind.

To help us consistently choose for centering prayer, we need to give it priority. It's that simple. Day in, day out, in all the busyness of life.

Key Points

• For a spiritual activity to become a supportive praxis that deepens our relationship with God, it needs to be practiced **regularly** and with **long-term commitment.**

• When starting a new praxis, let's be aware of mental or emotional games we can play with ourselves that may lead us to stop the new praxis. These include (but are certainly not limited to) feelings of **shame**, **guilt**, and **frustration.**

Connecting to Your Praxis

• What would a centering prayer praxis look like for you? How often per day or week could you show up for centering prayer? How long could each centering prayer session be for you?

_____

_____

_____

_____

_____

• What in your life may get in the way of a regular and long-term commitment to centering prayer?

_____

_____

_____

_____

_____

• Where would you practice centering prayer? What do you need for that space to be like?

_____

_____

_____

_____

_____

_____

_____

_____

2

WHERE DOES CENTERING PRAYER FIT?

THE SMALL BRASS BOWL sits in the hand of the meditation leader. She takes a smoothly carved wooden mallet and strikes the bowl once. The single, high-pitched tone breaks the silence of the room, ringing out and filling the air with sound that slowly dissipates and gives over once again to silence. The meditation has officially begun. I bring attention to all the actions I experience inside my body and mind. As an awareness arises, I name it. As a thought arises, I say to myself, "thinking." As a feeling arises, I say to myself, "feeling." As I hear a bird singing, I say to myself, "hearing." And so it goes until I hear the sound of the mallet against the brass bowl once again and the gentle tone filling the silence of the meditation space. I take a deep breath and slowly open my eyes.

The scene described on the previous page gives insight into what the practitioner is actually doing while seated in the contemplative practice of meditation. To an observer, the person seated in centering prayer as presented in the opening scene of the previous chapter and the person seated in meditation look like they're doing the same activity. However, the internal experience is quite different. It's important to acknowledge this fact as we explore how contemplative practices differ and where centering prayer actually fits in the mix.

In today's world of rapid communication and sensory overload, subtle yet important differences in meaning between terms and expressions can easily get blurred. For the general population, this is often the case with expressions like *meditation*, *prayer*, *contemplative prayer*, and of course, *centering prayer*. This conflating of terms often leads to using one term interchangeably for another. This can create confusion among those seeking out a spiritual praxis. Such confusion can quickly spiral into misinformation and even lead to institutional or individual protests against centering prayer.

Another danger that can arise from a blurring of terms and a lack of precision in the use of these terms is the practice of spiritual bypassing. This happens when a person uses religion or spiritual practices to avoid feeling emotions that make them uncomfortable or something other than happy. Some types of contemplative practices can be manipulated to accomplish this, often unconsciously. Knowing this and then spending a little time getting clear about how each of these practices differs can help us be more aware if we're engaging in spiritual bypassing.

Additionally, and in the spirit of education and clarity, we who engage in centering prayer need to count ourselves as knowledgeable emissaries for it. To be informed advocates of centering prayer, getting clear about what it is, particularly in relation to other spiritual practices, will help us speak in an accurate and clear fashion with the hope of raising people's awareness and interest in this valuable form of prayer. It's completely orthodox, wholly experiential, and tenderly nourishes our subjective relationship with God.

To that end, it's good to spend a little time to orient centering prayer in the larger landscape of contemplative practices.

Contemplative Practices

On the whole, the label *contemplative practices* can be applied to a broad category of sometimes similar and sometimes very different practices. The most obvious and shared characteristic of all of these practices is that each is an activity done in silence to focus awareness on self, mind, environment, or spirit.

Meditation

Meditation is widespread today, offering people an abundance of styles to choose from. Some styles (mindfulness or secular meditation, for example) have even been embraced by much of

21

western medicine and have an end goal of reducing stress. Other styles come from philosophical or religious traditions, including Christianity. Again, depending on the particular style or type of meditation, the technique and purpose can vary.

A cursory look at only a handful of different styles of meditation from some non-Christian traditions helps underscore this fact. Vipassana meditation, for example, is a Buddhist meditation that helps practitioners develop awareness of the activities of the mind. Tonglen meditation (also Buddhist) can be used to develop compassion in the heart of the practitioner. Yogic meditation (broadly speaking) is practiced to quiet the senses and encourage single-pointed focus. At the end of the day, much of meditation is generally concerned with experiencing the mind directly, without thoughts coloring that experience.

Christian Meditation

Meditation from a Christian perspective has a different flavor and is characterized by a searching or an inquiry. While practicing Christian meditation, one engages with God, primarily through God's Word, to understand deeper meanings and to experience a conversion of heart.

Within Christianity itself, there are a number of approaches or techniques to meditation. One particularly helpful example can be found in the contemplative practice known as *lectio divina*. This is a four-step praxis that includes Christian meditation as one of its steps.

1. *lectio* (reading)

2. *meditatio* (meditation)

3. *oratio* (prayer)

4. *contemplatio* (contemplation)

The second step in *lectio divina* focuses on meditation and traditionally follows seven to ten minutes of slowly reading from the Bible. The reader then chooses a sentence or phrase that stands out to meditate on.

When moving into this meditation step, one is encouraged to be receptive to the light of understanding that the Holy Spirit shines on the sentence or phrase taken from the Bible reading. Actual instructions can vary; however, one way is to begin by repeating the phrase in the mind, even over the course of the day, letting it start to take root. As this repetition takes place, the practitioner starts to observe their own life in relation to the phrase. This is not done in a rushed or anxious way. To the contrary, the practitioner softens the mind (giving judgment a rest) and allows the Holy Spirit to open their heart to a new awareness and to give insight to the practitioner.

Though it appears to start out as a mental activity through the repeating of the phrase, meditation can transform into an affective experience of the heart, moving the practitioner into a passive or contemplative realm.

Contemplative Prayer

With two thousand years of history under its belt, Christianity through the centuries has developed a host of definitions for prayer, which can be both beautiful and overwhelming as the definitions have been colored by different spiritualities and personalities within Christianity up and down the ages.

To start, let's look at the latest edition of *The Book of Common Prayer* (BCP) of the Episcopal Church. The BCP defines prayer as "responding to God, by thought and by deeds, with or without words." While this definition of prayer may seem quite basic at first blush, it's a rich starting point. However, because it's so unadorned, it can become easy to lose sight of the importance of what the definition's simple words communicate. They present prayer as a necessary foundation, without which we have no life, no relationship, no covenant with God. This orientation of prayer is breathtaking, and calls us to take a moment and let its simple but provocative message sink into our bodies and minds and hearts.

To this simple yet bold definition, we can add that Christian prayer has come to be seen as having three different expressions: vocal, meditative, and contemplative. For our current exploration, we'll focus on the contemplative expression of prayer, which is also known as contemplative prayer.

This particular expression of prayer starts to unfold as we move from our mind, our words, and our rational or intellectual thinking faculties towards the realm of just being. In contemplative prayer, we accept that at some point our thinking, or thinking in general, reaches its limit. At that point, we simply listen in order to be able to respond to God "without words," as the BCP suggests.

Just as meditation has different forms or styles, contemplative prayer does as well, though some of these styles are more nuanced and perhaps fall more appropriately under the heading of technique. With the understanding that contemplative prayer is at the opposite end of the contemplative practices spectrum from meditation, we can examine one of contemplative prayer's primary expressions: centering prayer.

Centering Prayer

Let's begin by recalling that centering prayer is actually prayer, and uniquely Christian, at that. Perhaps it's obvious that it's an expression of prayer, given its name. But it certainly bears repeating. It's an important distinction and one that is not solely academic. It's a distinction that affects our disposition toward our praxis of centering prayer and may even affect our commitment to it.

How does this distinction actually affect our disposition? Let's agree that prayer is vital to developing and deepening our relationship with God. Then let's acknowledge that we actually desire such a relationship with God. This is important, particularly for those who are ready to begin or who are in the process of healing their religion or God wounds.

With these two understandings in place, we can easily see that our orientation towards centering prayer as actual prayer adds weight and importance as well as priority for making time for it, making time for Christ, in our day-to-day life. Alternatively, if we consider centering prayer simply as another mindfulness practice or an activity that minimizes God and our relationship with God, then commitment to a regular praxis will be difficult to come by and sustain.

At this point in our exploration of centering prayer, it's enough simply to place centering prayer in its proper context within the landscape of contemplative practices. Our exploration of centering prayer will continue to unfold in both details and practices in the remaining chapters of this book.

Key Points

• The **interior experience** of the practitioner of meditation will be vastly different from the person engaged in centering prayer.

• How we **orient** centering prayer in the landscape of contemplative practices affects our **disposition** toward centering prayer and our overall praxis.

• Getting clear about the different types of contemplative practices **dispels confusion** and **supports a committed praxis.**

• Clarity allows us to speak informatively to others as **emissaries** for centering prayer and helps us **avoid spiritual bypassing.**

• Christian prayer can be **vocal, meditative**, and **contemplative.**

• *Contemplative practices* is a broad category that contains many styles of **meditation** and **contemplative prayer.**

• **Centering prayer** is a type of **Christian contemplative prayer.** It differs primarily from Christian meditation in that it is **not based on inquiry**.

Connect to Your Praxis

• Which contemplative practice(s) have you experienced?

_____

_____

_____

_____

_____

• How do you think being clear about the different types of contemplative practices will support your commitment to a centering prayer praxis?

_____

_____

_____

_____

• Why are you drawn toward centering prayer?

_____

_____

_____

_____

3

THE CENTERING OF CENTERING PRAYER

THE VERY CONCEPT OF prayer implies relationship with God. Each time we enter into prayer, regardless of its expression, we deepen that relationship. No matter where our prayer takes place externally, be it in church or at home or some other place out in the world, internally prayer is always an intimate experience with God.

That leaves us asking a related question: *Where internally is the place that intimacy with God in prayer unfolds?*

Scripture tells us that we should go into our inner room and shut the door. In one manner of interpretation, those words instruct us to turn inward as we pray because that is where we will find God during our prayer. Let's use this interpretation of that instruction from the Gospel of Matthew as a starting point for the internal *where* of centering prayer.

Perhaps before the question of *where* forms, a curiosity that may even be colored with a little confusion arises around the very name *centering prayer*. This curiosity/confusion can leave us with questions such as *What is centering?* and *What does it have to do with this type of prayer?*

The word *centering*, in this context, is a nod to both location and action. The location being referred to is the heart, though not necessarily the organ in our body known as the heart. Let's take a more poetic approach and understand *heart* as referring to our deepest self, that place within each of us that historically has been thought of as being located in the region of the heart, the very core or center of our being. We can use this understanding to build on the instruction from Matthew's Gospel.

Next, let's look at the action being disclosed through the use of the word *centering*. When we center ourselves, we bring our awareness as fully as possible to a particular location. During centering prayer, we move our awareness to that core place deep within the center of our body in a very conscious, unforced, and full way.

In the Heart

According to Holy Scripture, Christ lives in our heart, and it is the Holy Spirit that truly knows our heart. Scripture also tells us that our heart, that inmost part of ourself which is most often below the level of consciousness, is what prays.

As we move our awareness to our heart, we may sense that the prayer which takes place in secret in our inner room has already begun, seemingly without us. At times, it can feel like we're dropping into a conversation. Sometimes we drop into the middle of a sentence; sometimes we drop into a pause.

What we soon come to understand is that this prayer of our heart is actually unceasing. It's like a river flowing, a stream of ongoing communication between God and our deepest self. This bears witness to the mystery of prayer and, in particular, centering prayer. However, through our praxis of centering prayer, we not only become aware of this "conversation," but we can even consciously take part in this intimate and eternal prayer of the heart.

Key Points

• Prayer is an expression of relationship with God.

• Centering prayer unfolds in our inner room, which we understand as being our heart space.

• The centering of centering prayer refers to bringing our awareness to our heart space.

• Through centering prayer we can discover an intimate and unceasing prayer of the heart between our deepest self and God.

Connect to Your Praxis

• What stands out for you in the presentation of centering prayer in this chapter?

_____

_____

_____

_____

_____

• How will this understanding of centering prayer affect your commitment to it as a spiritual praxis?

_____

_____

_____

_____

_____

_____

_____

_____

4

The Dynamics of Centering Prayer

Any given centering prayer experience involves interior, non-physical movement akin to energy shifts or dynamics. It may be helpful to consider these energy shifts as periods of thought activity or feelings that move through the interior space of the mind and heart. They can be turbulent and rowdy or peaceful and calm. Each dynamic has its own "energetic signature," its own type of movement.

Our experience of centering prayer will be governed, in part, by these dynamics as they move across our interior landscape. It's important to know how to relate to and work with them, and Psalm 62 can serve as our guide. Its illuminating words will offer useful instructions about these dynamics that we'll face during each centering prayer experience.

Psalm 62

Psalm 62 is a profoundly heartfelt declaration about God; however, it can also be approached as a steadied, wisdom-filled treatise on centering prayer–one that is as vulnerable and intimate as it is insightful. When approaching Psalm 62 as an illuminating set of instructions, we find that it offers valuable glimpses of the dynamics of centering prayer's interior landscape.

To begin this approach to Psalm 62, it's helpful to understand the psalm's structure as it applies to centering prayer.

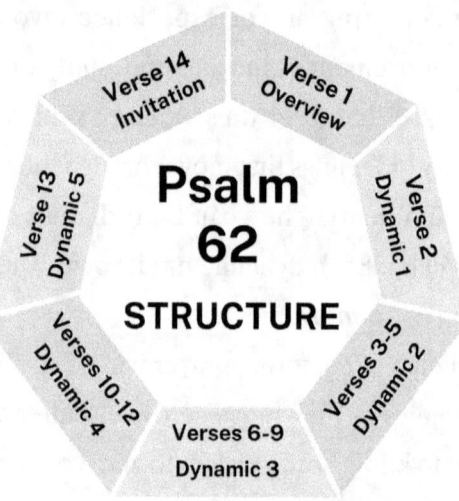

As you can see from the illustration on page 34, a certain set of verses (instructions) from the psalm focuses on each dynamic. The psalm begins with an overview in verse 1, then moves through five dynamics, and ends with an invitation in its final verse (14).

Before launching into a closer examination of the structure of Psalm 62, let's keep in mind that each experience of centering prayer will be different. Each person has a different relationship with God, and that relationship will unfold and deepen in a uniquely personal way in centering prayer. Therefore, we'll be examining centering prayer's structure as presented in Psalm 62 as a template that will be customized by the Holy Spirit.

Another note to keep in mind as we move through an exploration of the dynamics presented in Psalm 62 is that much more detail will be brought out in the subsequent chapters, when we examine the psalm verse by verse, and in some cases half verse by half verse. However, at this point, a study of the psalm's structure will allow for a broad understanding of the different energetic shifts that one may experience within centering prayer.

Psalm 62 is presented on the following page. Slowly read through its verses, letting the words wash over you. If you notice certain thoughts, emotions, or feelings start to show up in your body and mind as you read it, let them move into your awareness without trying to change them. Just notice them.

Psalm 62

1   For God Alone my soul in silence waits;
    from him comes my salvation

2   He alone is my rock and my salvation,
    my stronghold, so that I shall not be greatly shaken.

3   How long will you assail me to crush me, all you together,
    as if you were a leaning fence, a toppling wall?

4   They seek only to bring me down from my place of honor;
    lies are their chief delight.

5   They bless with their lips,
    but in their hearts they curse.

6   For God alone my soul in silence waits;
    truly, my hope is in him.

7   He alone is my rock and my salvation,
    my stronghold, so that I shall not be shaken.

8   In God is my safety and my honor;
    God is my strong rock and my refuge.

9   Put your trust in him always, O people,
    pour out your hearts before him, for God is our refuge.

10   Those of high degree are but a fleeting breath,
    even those of low estate cannot be trusted.

11   On the scales they are lighter than a breath,
    all of them together.

12   Put no trust in extortion; in robbery take no empty pride;
    though wealth increase, set not your heart upon it.

13   God has spoken once, twice have I heart it,
    that power belongs to God.

14   Steadfast love is yours, O Lord,
    for you repay everyone according to his deeds.

The Overview (verse 1)

This verse sets the tone and presents a big-picture look at what the psalm is about. It also states what centering prayer is and gives the ultimate reason to make it part of our lives.

Dynamic 1 (verse 2)

This single verse introduces us to the dynamic found at the beginning or genesis point of each centering prayer experience, which also serves as an anchor point for us as we find ourselves experiencing the other dynamics that flow through centering prayer.

Dynamic 2 (verses 3-5)

These verses present us with a glimpse at one of the internal dynamics or movements that we face each time we begin centering prayer. A cursory examination of the verbs used in the verses of this dynamic makes it obvious that activity or movement does take place in centering prayer. These verses also shine light on some of the feelings and thoughts that color this dynamic and that may lead to our being shaken, which has been foreshadowed at the end of verse 2.

Dynamic 3 (verses 6-9)

With verse 6, we enter into the third dynamic. If we read verse 6, we'll notice that it repeats the first line (verse 1a) of the psalm. We could refer to this dynamic as the Grand Return as it points to the moment in our centering prayer when we'll return to that anchor point and rediscover the internal silence that manifests as we again settle back into waiting for God.

Dynamic 4 (verses 10-12)

These verses suggest a time in centering prayer when we will experience the potential for more turbulent movement. However, when comparing the tone of these verses with those from Dynamic 2 (also a dynamic of rowdy movement), we actually perceive substantially less turbulence, less charge. This gives us opportunity to gain surer footing and clearer awareness as we realize that the energetic movements in this dynamic are not as upending as we may have feared.

Dynamic 5 (verse 13)

Now, the final dynamic brings us once again to a place of quiet where we can know that power belongs to God and not to the potentially destabilizing dynamics that we may have experienced up to this point.

Invitation (verse 14)

This final verse not only instructs but invites us to move into deeper relationship. It's an invitation to move through all that is gauzy and without substance (despite feeling perhaps quite the opposite) and into that which singularly possesses real substance: the reality that we call the love of God.

The Value of the Bird's Eye View

As we become familiar with these dynamics of centering prayer expressed through the structure of Psalm 62, we gain a bird's eye view of the internal movements and experiences of the praxis. We can, in turn, use this information, even as broadly as it has been presented so far, to disarm the three common impediments (shame, guilt, and frustration) that may get in the way of a regular centering prayer praxis over an extended period of time.

Ponder that last sentence a moment. Reflect on how big it is to know that the power that these three energetics may wield over us gets diminished exponentially simply by being aware of the interior movements and dynamics of centering prayer.

If we understand that centering prayer isn't interiorly static and that its interior movement isn't necessarily linear nor identical each time, then we'll be well prepared and equipped to diffuse any power plays that these three energetics may engage us in as they try to destabilize our commitment to centering prayer.

Additionally, in regard to safeguarding our commitment to centering prayer, it can be pivotal to remember that sustaining our praxis so that it can sustain us comes down to consciously choosing to spend time with God in centering prayer. We're not showing up for ourselves alone, which could be considered selfish or even transactional. Instead, we're showing up for our relationship with God. We're showing up because God and God's overflowing love for us are at the center of life. Centering prayer is a way for us to taste that reality continuously, and in tasting it, we will be transformed.

Key Points

• Psalm 62 can be approached as a heartfelt set of instructions for centering prayer.

• Its structure provides a bird's eye view of the dynamics of our inner experience of centering prayer.

• The psalm's structure includes an overview of centering prayer, introduces the five dynamics of interior activity of centering prayer, and concludes with an invitation to a deeper relationship with God through a sustained praxis of centering prayer.

• During each praxis period, the dynamics of centering prayer may occur over and over again. However, they may not be experienced linearly. It's also good to know that they may not all appear in every centering prayer experience.

• Day in and day out, we must make a conscious choice to spend time with God through centering prayer. It's this conscious choice on our part that sustains a centering prayer praxis that sustains us over time.

Connect to Your Praxis

• Note particular experiences in your life that may trigger guilt, shame, or frustration with centering prayer.

_____

_____

_____

_____

_____

• How do the dynamics presented in Psalm 62 mirror your thought movements outside of centering prayer?

_____

_____

_____

_____

• Describe the value you perceive in making centering prayer part of your life.

_____

_____

_____

_____

5

THE SENSES OF SCRIPTURE

To set the stage for our exploration of Psalm 62 as a series of instructions or counsel for centering prayer, we'll need to consider the lenses that Christian Tradition uses to interpret Holy Scripture. Each of these ways of seeing is called a sense.

Literally Speaking

There are two broad categories of senses for interpretation. One is the literal sense and the other is the spiritual sense.

The literal sense is quite simply what it sounds like. The meaning of the scripture is conveyed in a straightforward manner by the words that have been recorded. Of course, despite the straightforward nature of the literal sense or lens, a little more is asked of the reader than just reading the words and taking them for face value as they appear on the page.

In order to arrive at a proper literal interpretation, we need to understand which literary form the text is. For example, is the text a poem, a myth, or an historical narrative (as historical writing was understood at the time)?

This is important to take into account because each type of literary form expresses truth using literary devices proper to that form. For example, poetry often takes advantage of symbolism and metaphor while myth creates a tale to illustrate a basic truth.

Spiritually Speaking

Contrasting the literal sense is the spiritual sense, which is less about a surface reading of the text and more about a closer reading of the text. As such, the realities and events within Holy Scripture can be seen as signs or symbols pointing to a deeper meaning or expression of truth. Tradition has divided the spiritual sense into three subcategories: the allegorical, the moral, and the anagogical.

Briefly put, the allegorical sense is used to relate events in the Old Testament to the New Testament in order to anchor them and show their significance in Christ. The moral sense helps us interpret scripture so that we may act more in alignment with the teachings of Christ. The anagogical sense interprets scripture in a way that points us towards our future in Christ.

Our Approach to Sense

We'll most often use the literal sense to interpret Psalm 62. Since we know that the psalms are poetry or hymns, we also know that this type of literature is often filled with symbolism. It's through the lens of symbolism that we'll discover and interpret Psalm 62's set of instructions for centering prayer.

These instructions, however, are not a set of directions that show the steps for centering prayer. In other words, they're not like a booklet of directions that would illustrate how to assemble a piece of furniture. Instead, the instructions found in Psalm 62 shine light on the dynamics of centering prayer and point toward how experience may unfold while in centering prayer.

Key Points

• Christian Tradition uses particular lenses (known as *senses*) to interpret Holy Scripture.

• The two main lenses that Tradition has used through the ages are the literal lens and the spiritual lens.

• The literal lens is a more straightforward reading of Holy Scripture based on the particular type of literature we're reading (e.g., The Psalms or Chapter 6 in The Gospel of Mark).

• Different types of literature (literary form) express truth using literary devices proper to their form.

• The spiritual lens interprets Holy Scripture as containing signs that point toward a deeper meaning.

• We'll use the literal sense to interpret Psalm 62, approaching it as poetry containing certain literary devices such as symbolism.

Connect to Your Praxis

• If this is the first time you've heard that the Bible is made up of different types of literature, describe how that lands with you. If you knew about this fact prior to reading this chapter, how has it influenced your approach to reading the Bible?

_____

_____

_____

_____

_____

_____

_____

_____

_____

_____

• How do you feel about the use of different interpretive senses to discern the meaning of Holy Scripture?

_____

_____

_____

_____

_____

• How open are you at this moment to the idea of using the literal sense to interpret Psalm 62?

_____

_____

_____

_____

_____

• If there is hesitation on your part, how can you be with that hesitation without it causing you to discount the value of the instructions presented in Psalm 62?

_____

_____

_____

_____

_____

_____

_____

_____

_____

PSALM 62

INSTRUCTIONS FOR CENTERING PRAYER

CENTERING PRAYER

These are the basic steps for centering prayer. These steps will be adjusted slightly throughout the book according to each particular instruction from Psalm 62.

1	**SIT** In a quiet and calm space, sit comfortably. This can be on the floor, on a cushion, or in a chair. Remember that if you need to adjust your seat while in centering prayer, you can.
2	**CLOSE YOUR EYES** Simply close your eyes once you find yourself seated comfortably.
3	**SETTLE INTO YOUR BODY** Take a few deep breaths in and out through your nose, and notice how your body is showing up. With each breath, let your body relax into its seated posture.
4	**REST IN YOUR HEART SPACE WITH AWARENESS** Move your awareness to your heart area. Notice any sensations. This is where your centering prayer takes place. Continue to be present to all that shows up.
5	**SLOWLY OPEN YOUR EYES** As your centering prayer session comes to a close, bring your awareness to your breath, then to the whole of your body. After a few breaths, slowly open your eyes.

6

⁓⧈⁓

WORKING WITH THE
INSTRUCTIONS

As WE MOVE INTO the next section of the book and focus on the
substance of the verses of Psalm 62, we should take a moment
to explore how best to work with the information we unpack.

The left-hand page of each chapter opening contains a set of
centering prayer steps. These steps outline a way to bring each
instruction into our centering prayer experiences. That means
that each will be slightly different and nuanced according to the
particular instruction from the psalm. Readers may choose to
use these steps or not; however, those who are new to centering
prayer may find them to be of particular value because they offer
a somewhat progressive approach to developing a centering
prayer praxis.

Any number of ways exist to work with the instructions from
Psalm 62 and put them into action so that they come alive and

truly support a praxis. One way, for example, is to work with one chapter per day in the following manner.

1. Read the chapter, taking notes on those parts of the chapter that speak to you.

2. Use the *Instructions Drawn From the Psalm* section as a way to amplify your notes from the chapter.

3. Complete the questions for reflection, remembering that if you need more space you can write your answers in a journal.

4. Endeavor to use the centering prayer steps that accompany the chapter for your personal centering prayer time.

5. If a chapter has an imagination-based experience, choose to spend ample time doing it either before or after your centering prayer experience.

While some may prefer to follow a format like the one above, devoting a single sitting to reading, reflecting, and then settling into centering prayer itself, it certainly isn't the only approach. Let time be the guide, remembering that it's better to adjust for time rather than rushing through each element in order to pack all of them into a single sitting. Also, it's important to remember that centering prayer should take priority and not be sacrificed in order to read a chapter or respond to the reflection questions.

Journaling is another activity that can be worthwhile as an accompaniment to a spiritual praxis like centering prayer. Keeping a journal is a way to bring awareness and clarity to our experiences. We may even have insightful epiphanies if we reread earlier journal entries.

While no hard and fast rules exist concerning what to write in a journal, some potential content options include answers to the reflection questions from this book and descriptions of experiences as your praxis unfolds. The one danger to be aware of is the lure of using the journal as a way to judge "progress" with centering prayer. Remember that journaling is about describing experiences from the process and not grading the progress.

Because healing religion and God wounds can be a layered process, keeping a journal may be particularly helpful for those on that path. Placing a journal and a pen nearby while reading this book or sitting in centering prayer can help capture the immediacy and freshness of thoughts and emotions and stories that bubble up from reading or that show up right after centering prayer.

CENTERING PRAYER

1	**SIT AND CLOSE YOUR EYES** In a quiet and calm space, sit and get comfortable. Then close your eyes.
2	**SETTLE INTO YOUR BODY** Take a few deep breaths through your nose as you become aware of your body.
3	**REPEAT THE PSALM'S FIRST LINE** Recall the first line of Psalm 62. Allow the words to wash over you as you slowly say each one. Linger on those words that you feel drawn to linger on.
4	**FEEL THE LONGING AS IT VIBRATES IN YOUR BODY** Notice your body. Become aware of where in your body the longing for God shows up. Notice the sensations, and feel how your body longs for God.
5	**REST IN YOUR HEART SPACE WITH EXPECTATION** Gently move your awareness to your heart area. Become aware of how your waiting feels. Be present to the sensations and to what shows up.
6	**SLOWLY OPEN YOUR EYES** As your centering prayer session comes to a close, bring your awareness to your breath, then to the whole of your body. After a few breaths, slowly open your eyes.

7

⎯⎯⎯✦⎯⎯⎯

FOR GOD ALONE
MY SOUL IN SILENCE
WAITS

IT WAS POINTED OUT in Chapter 5 that a psalm is a type of poetry or hymn. As such, it may be helpful to remember that the text of each psalm appears as a number of verses, and each verse usually (and quite logically) contains two half verses. For example, verse 1a and verse 1b make up the complete first verse in this psalm. One other structural characteristic of this psalm to note is that each half verse appears as its own line of text.

As Psalm 62 opens, the psalmist wastes no time in revealing a show-stopping overview of centering prayer. More precisely, in this first half verse, he proclaims in a pithy yet elegant style the central action that takes place during centering prayer: *For God alone my soul in silence waits.*

For God Alone

With these three words, the psalmist declares, in a clear and unambiguous way, what we should expect as we enter into centering prayer: an encounter with God. It's as if the psalmist gives voice to a clarion call springing forth from our whole being, waking us up to our thirst for a real relationship with God. As we begin this journey into centering prayer, we would do well to let these three words pierce the veneer of the myriad daily and mundane activities that we have been using to attempt to silence this longing in our heart.

This proclamation is not so much a demand as it is an assent to our faith in God and our trust that God will arrive. For our part, we make good on that assent by consciously choosing to show up for centering prayer rather than choosing to do some other activity from our daily life. These three words, when heard in this layered fashion, set the stage in a compelling way for our interior experience.

Centering prayer is always about surrendering to God. When our hearts cry out with *for God alone*, we are, in effect, acknowledging our willingness to surrender, to give over to God during our centering prayer. This interior surrendering then reverberates out to the whole of our life as assent to live for God rather than to live selfishly for ourselves.

Let's linger a moment or two with the word *alone.* It has the power to convey the intensity of our desire for God. Take a moment to ponder that.

Settle into your body and feel that magnitude of desire actually vibrating in the very cells of your body.

God is so precious and so vital to the soul that nothing else can fulfill the soul's longing. Nothing else has the power to so completely and fully give rest, ease, and comfort to us, to our souls. We may know this intellectually, but dropping into our body with awareness gives us the opportunity to experience this longing that is actually pulsing through our body.

My Soul in Silence

The silence of centering prayer is not an empty void. On the contrary, the silence of centering prayer is the holy ground of intimacy. It is in this silence that everything fades away except our relationship with God alone. Just our soul and God. It's in this silence that God sees us. It's in this silence that God tenderly looks into our eyes. It's in the intimacy of this silence that the gaze of God draws us close, embracing us in love. In this holy silence, our soul opens to receive God's embrace.

During centering prayer, we can actually begin to feel a love rising up in our hearts. Perhaps it's a subtle sensation at first. If so, be gentle with it, without forcing it to be any certain way, and quite naturally that flame of love will grow. This is a love that assures us that God sees us, that God counts us worthy, and that God loves us beyond measure.

This is the richness of the silence of centering prayer.

Waits

Our waiting in centering prayer is an action that underscores our faith and trust that God will show up. That being the case, one important take-away from this first line of the psalm is that we truly do have faith and trust in God, even if we don't acknowledge it consciously each day or even if we deny it on some level internally or to others. The very fact that we are choosing to wait in centering prayer also points toward an acknowledgement that we're in relationship with God. It's worth noting that this relationship we're acknowledging is not simply theoretical. It's experiential, and we're living it out each time we sit in centering prayer.

If we agree that centering prayer is an experience of being in relationship with God, then this waiting spoken of by the psalmist is not inconsequential. It serves as an anchor and provides a certain stability for our praxis. Why is this important? Because as we wait, as we anchor ourselves in centering prayer, the waiting provides the opportunity for our presence and awareness of each moment to manifest in our consciousness. This is big, as we'll come to understand in the following chapters.

In short, our waiting is not a passive experience during which we zone out or become impatient as can so often happen in our exterior life. Instead, this waiting opens up a landscape of awareness within us, a "place" where we can be fully present with God.

Instructions Drawn From the Psalm

• We should expect an encounter with God during our centering prayer experience.

• We would not entertain this expectation if we didn't already have faith and trust in God, which is the foundation of relationship.

• The silence of centering prayer is not an empty void.

• This silence is the holy ground of intimacy between God and each of us. It's rich with encounter.

• The waiting we do in centering prayer is further confirmation of our faith and trust in God.

• Our waiting is not passive. It's a conscious action that opens up a "place" for us to be with God.

Reflect

• Set aside your initial reaction to hearing the sometimes overused phrase "my personal relationship with Christ (God)." Then describe your relationship with Christ at present.

_____

_____

_____

_____

• Describe the level of your faith and of your trust in God.

_____

_____

_____

• How do they affect your relationship with God?

_____

_____

_____

_____

· How have you ordered your life in relation to God?

_____

_____

_____

_____

_____

· Describe how the concept of internal silence presented in this chapter lands with you.

_____

_____

_____

_____

· Why have you committed to a centering prayer praxis?

_____

_____

_____

_____

CENTERING PRAYER

1
SIT AND CLOSE YOUR EYES
In a quiet and calm space, sit and get comfortable. Then close your eyes.

2
SETTLE INTO YOUR BODY
Take a few deep breaths through your nose as you become aware of your body.

3
REPEAT THE PSALM'S SECOND LINE
Recall the second line of Psalm 62: *From Him comes...* Slowly say each word. Linger on those words that you feel drawn to linger on.

4
FEEL BEING DRAWN INTO ALIGNMENT WITH GOD
Notice your body. Become aware of being drawn into alignment with God. Notice the sensations, and feel how your body is showing up for God.

5
REST IN YOUR HEART SPACE WITH EXPECTATION
Gently move your awareness to your heart area. Become aware of how your waiting feels. Be present to the sensations and to what shows up.

6
SLOWLY OPEN YOUR EYES
As your centering prayer session comes to a close, bring your awareness to your breath, then to the whole of your body. After a few breaths, slowly open your eyes.

8

From Him Comes My Salvation

FOR SOME, LIKE ME, hearing certain words freely and liberally batted around the Christian ethos can give the impression that people are communicating in a secret code, one that leaves me feeling like I'm the only one not getting the meaning of these words. Of course, the fact that I'm a bit of a language nerd most likely contributes to this feeling in me. Regardless of why this feeling arises, I actually do realize that I'm not the only one plagued by it.

Take the word *salvation* that appears in this second line of Psalm 62 as an example. I have a general idea of its meaning; however, it is used so frequently that I often wonder how many people just say it without actually understanding the depth of its meaning and what, in this case, it means for our centering prayer instruction and praxis.

The dictionary definition of *salvation* is "a deliverance from harm or ruin." In Christianity, salvation is a deliverance from the sin and the harm (or ruin) experienced as a result of sin. There's a lot there, not to mention that another one of "those" words crops up in context with *salvation*. That other word is *sin*.

In the Nicene Creed, we confess that Christ came down from heaven for our salvation, reconciling us with God. On the surface, this may appear rather formulaic and recited so often as to lose much of its impact. However, if we consider these words more closely, we realize that salvation is more than a deliverance (which is big, in and of itself). Salvation is at its core about reconciling us with God; it's about restoring our relationship with God through the forgiveness of sins.

Sin, Forgiveness, and Salvation

Over the next several chapters, we'll spend some time exploring liberating concepts of *sin* and *forgiveness* and *salvation*, and how they work together in our centering prayer praxis. That means we'll focus on how *we* work with them during centering prayer, with the intention of deepening our relationship with God.

Let's begin by looking at the word *sin*. To say that it's a loaded word is quite the understatement. For many, the word *sin* shows up with lots of baggage. The word has been (and still is) weaponized by many to judge and to scapegoat and to control. It's not often presented in a context of love, at least not in one that is healthy. However, if we are to deepen our relationship with God, we need to reframe the word to present the concept of sin in a more authentic and non-threatening way: one that builds up our centering prayer praxis.

One of the less threatening definitions is one of the more precise translations from Koine Greek. It presents the idea of sin as a missing of the mark. Take a moment and reflect on that idea. Notice how it lands in your body.

Then let's add a little nuance to that idea by looking at the concept of sin as action or thought that moves us out of alignment with God.

Here's why this matters. When we're out of alignment with God, we have a more difficult time consciously receiving God's love and support, which often has a domino effect and moves us still further out of alignment and out of relationship with God. In short, this reframing also identifies sin as a force that has consequences.

If we start to understand that our actions and thoughts can have this kind of effect on our relationship with God, we can also start to let go of the unhealthy baggage (shame and/or guilt, etc.) that often travels with the word *sin*, particularly with more surface or generic definitions of *sin*. When we let go of that baggage, we receive the opportunity not just to gain clarity around how we choose *for* or *against* our relationship (alignment) with God. We also create the space to choose with more ease to be in alignment with God. Can you see how liberating and empowering that is?

Beyond the Baggage

Reading the second line from Psalm 62 while starting to imbibe this healthier understanding of *sin*, we create the space to glimpse a deep truth about God, one that often gets forgotten or, even worse, discarded as fiction. The deep truth is this: God invites us to be in a real, life-giving, intimate relationship, now, in this very moment, and for eternity.

If I sit with that awareness, even for a short time, it starts to overwhelm me in the same way that standing on top of a mountain and taking in the majesty of the expanse of grandeur before me does. Then, as I let this verse sink into my heart, I'm gently drawn into that space of intimacy with God, where God invites me into relationship. And it's total gift, offered freely and generously and vulnerably, the way one lover would offer himself or herself in relationship to another.

Tying this back to centering prayer, how precious the opportunity we have to be able to consciously sit in this very intimate space within the silence of our heart with God, with the one who, like a single-hearted and devoted lover, only wants to spend time with us, and who craves to bring us into an ever-deepening relationship.

Instructions Drawn From the Psalm

• Psalm 62 gives us insights to deepen our understanding of God. Here the psalmist affirms that God offers us salvation, that it flows from God.

• *Salvation* is joyful. For some, however, its joy may get covered over by wounds that linger from the effects of a legacy of weaponized concepts linked to *sin* and *forgiveness*.

• To start to recover the joy of *salvation*, we must embrace a healthier concept of *sin*. In its original Greek, *sin* conveys the idea of missing the mark. We can refine and reframe this less-triggering definition if we add nuance to it and consider *sin* as any action or thought that moves us out of alignment with God.

• With this healthier understanding of *sin* in place, we can start to appreciate the psalmist's words about the flow of salvation. We can begin to appreciate the deep truth that God invites us into a real, life-giving, intimate relationship, now, in this very moment, and for eternity.

Reflect

• What has been your understanding up to this point of *salvation*?

_____

_____

_____

_____

_____

• How has that understanding impacted your relationship with God?

_____

_____

_____

_____

• Before reading this chapter, how did you understand *sin*?

_____

_____

_____

_____

• How does the view of *sin* presented in this chapter land with you?

_____

_____

_____

_____

_____

• If you were to work with this chapter's idea of *sin*, how would it affect your relationship with God?

_____

_____

_____

_____

_____

_____

_____

_____

_____

CENTERING PRAYER

1	**SIT AND CLOSE YOUR EYES** In a quiet and calm space, sit and get comfortable. Then close your eyes.
2	**SETTLE INTO YOUR BODY** Take a few deep breaths through your nose as you become aware of your body.
3	**REPEAT THE PSALM'S THIRD LINE** Recall the third line of Psalm 62: *He alone is....* Slowly say each word. Linger on those words that you feel drawn to linger on.
4	**EXPERIENCE A LOVING STRENGTH FROM GOD** Notice your body. Become aware of a flow of loving strength from God. Notice the sensations, and feel how your body receives this strength.
5	**REST IN YOUR HEART SPACE WITH EXPECTATION** Gently move your awareness to your heart area. Become aware of how your waiting feels. Be present to the sensations and to what shows up.
6	**SLOWLY OPEN YOUR EYES** As your centering prayer session comes to a close, bring your awareness to your breath, then to the whole of your body. After a few breaths, slowly open your eyes.

9

<hr>

HE ALONE IS MY
ROCK AND MY
SALVATION

THIS IS A PIVOTAL line in the psalm: *He alone is my rock and my salvation.* For many, it may even be the very climax of the whole psalm. It's keenly worth noting that this line reveals an epiphany about our relationship with God.

He Alone Is

The initial three words of this line echo the first three words at the start of the psalm. This line's three initial words call us to acknowledge yet again how vital God is for us. It can be shocking to recognize just how often this rings hollow for many of us in our day-to-day lives. Such a recognition, shocking as it may be, can serve us by increasing our commitment to our centering prayer praxis.

Let's take a moment to consider the questions that these three words are asking each of us. These questions look something like this: *How do we orient our lives toward God? What holds primacy in our hearts? What gets in the way of our relationship with God?*

Regardless of the season of life we find ourselves in or what our commitments are, these questions are always begging us to look at where we find solid ground in this present moment. We need to assess which of our relationships is most important. That means, in part, we need to understand not only which relationship takes precedence but also why it holds the position that it does.

For each of us, the answers to these questions will be different. However, it's evident that the psalmist is unequivocally telling us with these three words that we would do well to give our relationship with God priority and primacy. This would then allow us to show up for others from a place of security, ushered in through our rightly ordered alignment with God. In short, when our relationship with God takes priority, we find ourselves being able to show up fully and authentically for our other relationships. As counterintuitive as that may seem to some people, orienting our life to God and through God causes the rest of life to line up and to fall into proper order.

My Rock

The use of the word *rock* here connotes strength and standing solidly and firmly in place, even being grounded and unflappable.

In English, for example, we have an expression that illustrates what the psalmist implies through the use of *my rock*. Here's a sentence with the expression: *She is my rock when I feel like my world is slipping away.*

The danger here, and it's worth pausing to determine if you believe this on some level, is to let the word *rock* morph into meaning "emotionless, uncaring, and stoic."

We also have the expressions in English *heart of rock* and *heart of stone*. These expressions are most often used to convey that a person has no empathy or doesn't feel emotion.

Given the range of expression that can be attached to *my rock* or *rock*, let's agree that the psalmist uses *He alone is my rock...* to refer to how God alone is always there for us and that God is our strength. Let's also work toward not attaching *uncaring* or *emotionless* or other similar adjectives to the psalmist's meaning.

My Salvation

This half verse ends with the word *salvation* again. This time, however, instead of repeating the previous half verse which states that my salvation *comes from* God, the psalmist tells us that *he (God) alone is...my salvation*. That's a big and important shift.

In particular, the psalmist points us toward a deeper understanding about God. Not only does my salvation flow from God, but God's very being is salvation. We have been led to some very holy ground with this revelation.

This abiding and inexhaustible love that is the very essence of God does something incomprehensible when it comes in contact with us. It actually dissipates (forgives) our sin. Being in the presence of God through our relationship with him both restores our alignment with God and makes way for us to experience the all-embracing, intimate love of God.

We'll get more into forgiveness in later chapters. In the meantime, here's an imagination-based experience for you to work with to start to bring this all into focus. Read each sentence slowly as you use all of your senses to imagine it.

You're in a field of darkness. It's daytime, but you can't see the sun, feel its warmth, or enjoy the streams of sunlight shining on your face. A thick, muffling fog surrounds and confuses you. The fog represents your sin; the sun is God; the sun's rays are God's love. As the rays of the sun touch the fog, it dissipates and burns off. Now, you find yourself surrounded by the radiance of the sun. You bask in its light and feel its warmth on your face and body, all as you take in the brilliance of the field where you stand.

Centering prayer ushers us into a salvific realm. It's what the psalmist attests to. That can come across as a bold claim, perhaps too bold even. However, experience bears it out. Experience bears witness to the restorative potential of centering prayer that is rooted in the simplicity of the surrendering and offering of our heart (and what is in our heart) to God.

Instruction Drawn From the Psalm

• The primacy of God, and as such our relationship with God, is clearly restated in this half verse. As we make our relationship with God the primary relationship in our life, everything becomes ordered properly.

• God is always there for us. We draw strength through our relationship with God. Knowing this in our mind is one thing, but getting a taste of it in our life helps us give priority to our relationship with God.

• We're told earlier in the psalm that our salvation comes from God. However, in this half verse, we're brought into a more intimate awareness. God's very being and essence is our salvation.

Reflect

• Consider your relationship with God. Describe where it fits into your life. How do you justify to yourself its position in your life?

_____

_____

_____

_____

_____

_____

_____

_____

• What in your life's experience stands out as evidence that God is always there for you as you live your life?

_____

_____

_____

_____

_____

• How do you gain strength from your relationship with God?

_____

_____

_____

_____

_____

• How does your drawing near to God or turning from God affect you and your life?

_____

_____

_____

_____

• Why do you choose at times to resist God's love?

_____

_____

_____

_____

CENTERING PRAYER

1	**SIT AND CLOSE YOUR EYES** In a quiet and calm space, sit and get comfortable. Then close your eyes.
2	**SETTLE INTO YOUR BODY** Take a few deep breaths through your nose as you become aware of your body.
3	**REPEAT THE PSALM'S FOURTH LINE** Recall the fourth line of Psalm 62: *my stronghold, so that I shall....* Slowly say each word. Linger on those words that you feel drawn to linger on.
4	**EXPERIENCE THE PROTECTION OF GOD** Notice your body. Become aware of sensations of safety and protection from God. Notice how you feel in your body as you stay with these sensations.
5	**REST IN YOUR HEART SPACE WITH EXPECTATION** Gently move your awareness to your heart area. Become aware of how your waiting feels. Be present to the sensations and to what shows up.
6	**SLOWLY OPEN YOUR EYES** As your centering prayer session comes to a close, bring your awareness to your breath, then to the whole of your body. After a few breaths, slowly open your eyes.

10

⌒⌒⌒⌒

MY STRONGHOLD...

VERSE 2B OF PSALM 62 reads *my stronghold, so that I shall not be greatly shaken.* It completes the thought started in the previous half verse. It also incorporates a bit of a cliffhanger. The psalmist's imagery in this cliffhanger opens a door for us to access a physical reference or experience that ties into the way that we reframed sin in Chapter 7.

Stronghold

In this half verse, the psalmist presents us with another word to describe God: *stronghold.* If we pause and consider this description, lots of images may come to mind. For example, it's easy to relate *stronghold* to an isolated fort deep in the wilds of the frontier or a castle surrounded with thick stone walls perched high on a hilltop.

The common denominator, of course, among these images is protection. A stronghold is a place that provides safety against the harshness of the wilderness and the invading forces that battle against those inside the stronghold.

While honoring the psalmist's choice of image to convey this quality of God, we once again need to be cautious about how our own wounds may unconsciously color the image and quality. For example, strength and protection can become imbued with ideas of fear or even punishment. As such, it's good to take a moment to notice what ideas you associate with or use to color the image of stronghold, particularly as it relates to this psalm, your current relationship with God or religion, and centering prayer.

At this point in the psalm, we're not yet told what God, being our stronghold, will protect us from. Of course, it's not too difficult to guess. After all, much exists in the big, bold, and beautiful world that could cause us to seek God as a stronghold. Despite not yet having been told, the words in the last part of this half verse shine light on *why* we need a stronghold: *so that I won't be greatly shaken.*

Greatly Shaken

The image of being greatly shaken is provocative and seizes our attention. It also corresponds or connects with how we reframed the definition of *sin*: a choice that brings us out of alignment with God. Let's remember that being greatly shaken can be the effect of such a choice, and it can be a cause that leads to a choice that moves us or keeps us out of alignment with God.

Think about driving a car with its wheels out of alignment. The vibrations from the misalignment cause a driver to be shaken and affect the driver's relationship with the car. Something similar can be experienced when we hear musical notes that don't create a pleasing harmony or someone singing off key. Depending on the level or range of the discord, we can feel it in our bodies and minds as a jarring or shaking. This may move us towards a decision never to listen to that song again.

A more psychological example takes place when events in life do not match our belief system or our expectations. We experience such situations as dissonance, shaking our minds and rippling out to our bodies, influencing how we choose to be in relationship with such situations.

Being shaken (mentally or emotionally) can disorient us, pushing us toward doubt or similar thoughts. Such experiences can then impact the future choices we make, possibly leading to actions that cause us to move out of alignment or harmony with God. The one aspect not factored into the examples above but that comes into play is how difficult it can be for us to choose consistently for alignment and harmony with God.

The psalmist, however, does give us a glimmer of hope by reminding us that we won't experience being *greatly shaken* when God is our stronghold.

It bears pointing out that we still may be shaken. However, it's also worth noting that the degree to which we are shaken is related to the degree to which God is our stronghold.

My...

Let's take a closer look at this little word *my*. In the complete second verse, we see it used three times: *my rock, my salvation, my stronghold*. That kind of repetition calls for attention and should ignite our curiosity. Why? In short, this little word is alerting us to something big and important: our particular relationship with God.

The psalmist is putting our relationship with God under a spotlight to help us see clearly and acknowledge the depth of our relationship with God in this moment. Is our relationship so deep and so intimate that we can freely call God *my rock, my salvation, my stronghold*?

It's easy to lay claim to this kind of relationship using only our minds. It's quite another thing to move it into our hearts, to experience and make choices in life based on a lived relationship with God that is so vulnerable that we can acknowledge that God is our rock, our salvation, and our stronghold.

Letting that sink in as we reflect on this verse allows for an honest awareness of where we are in our relationship with God. Reflecting on this also has the power to open space in our heart for a dynamic and ongoing relationship with God to unfold and be nurtured. Through this experience as well as through centering prayer, we come to understand that our relationship with God isn't static. It doesn't arrive at a final destination. Rather, our relationship with God is always evolving and deepening and ever fresh.

Instructions Drawn From the Psalm

• God is imbued with the qualities of dependability, strength, and safety.

• Taking refuge in God ensures peace of mind through centering prayer and as we move through life.

• Without making God and our relationship with God the foundation of our life, we can count on the ups and downs of life greatly shaking us.

• When we are greatly shaken by life, we more than likely make choices that move us further out of alignment and harmony with God.

Reflect

• Describe how taking refuge in God would or does look for you.

_____

_____

_____

_____

_____

_____

_____

• Spend some time reflecting on and describing the role that your relationship with God plays in your life.

_____

_____

_____

_____

_____

_____

_____

_____

• Give a few concrete examples as evidence.

_____

_____

_____

_____

_____

_____

_____

• What relationships or experiences do you look to or fall back on when life "greatly shakes" you?

_____

_____

_____

_____

_____

_____

_____

_____

_____

_____

CENTERING PRAYER

1

SIT AND CLOSE YOUR EYES
In a quiet and calm space, sit either on the floor, on a cushion, or in a chair. Get comfortable. Close your eyes.

2

SETTLE INTO YOUR BODY
Take a few deep breaths through your nose. Allow yourself to become aware of your body as you say to yourself "For God alone my soul in silence waits."

3

BREATHE INTO YOUR HEART SPACE
Shift your awareness to your breath. Let your breath be the vehicle that moves your awareness into your heart space.

4

OPEN YOUR HEART SPACE
As your awareness moves into your heart space, allow that space to open more and more with each gentle inhalation.

5

REST IN YOUR HEART SPACE WITH EXPECTATION
Allow your awareness to expand slightly from your heart space until you notice subtle sensations like butterflies in your stomach. This is your Holy Ground. Rest here in waiting.

6

SLOWLY OPEN YOUR EYES
As your centering prayer session comes to a close, bring your awareness to your breath, then to the whole of your body. After a few breaths, slowly open your eyes.

11

〜⤫〜

CHECKING IN

THE FIRST TWO VERSES of Psalm 62, as we have seen, give us much
to consider about our relationship with God. The first verse
not only tells us what centering prayer is and why we should
make it our praxis, it also draws us into reflection about our God
and our relationship with God. We're drawn more deeply into
that reflection through verse 2, which exposes the first dynamic
of the internal activity of centering prayer. This verse as an
instruction gives us our anchor point as we close our eyes and
begin our centering prayer experience.

It's helpful to remember that centering prayer is not a prayer
of the mind. It's not like meditation or discursive prayer that
tends to unfold completely in the mind. Centering prayer is
about moving into and experiencing the reality of our heart.
This can be a big jump for some people. It can also be a new
experience for others. Regardless of which camp you land in,
centering prayer is a humbling equalizer. As we explore deep-

ening our centering prayer praxis and, in turn, healing through our wounds as we deepen our relationship with God, we're all going to be entering pristine territory with new experiences.

Centering prayer takes us to a space in our heart where we wait for God. In this waiting, we come to experience God's love as an invitation to be in (deeper) relationship. Through our assent or acceptance of that invitation, we gain clarity as we come to understand from a heart space that to be in relationship with God is our very salvation. It's where we find life.

A Note About Waiting and the Heart

In the spirit of giving experiential validity to the instructions found in this psalm, let's engage in an experience of waiting, as we're invited to participate in during centering prayer. You may want to read through the following italicized paragraphs until you're familiar with the process. Then you can close your eyes and guide yourself through the experience without having to interrupt it to read the next step.

As you close your eyes and settle into your body, begin to move your awareness gently to your heart space. Sometimes this can feel as if you have walked into a dark room from the bright sunshine, and you need to give your eyes a moment to become accustomed to the light. That's how moving into your heart space at the beginning of centering prayer can feel at times, and it's okay to take a moment or two to orient yourself.

To adjust to this new space, take a few moments to breathe and to settle and to notice. As you settle in and scan your heart space, you'll come to notice a feeling. It's a bit difficult to describe, but it's similar to having butterflies in your stomach. This is what you can call a Holy Feeling. This feeling may be subtle at first; however, if you stay with it, without forcing it, you'll notice that it blossoms into more fullness. You'll sense that this Holy Feeling is like a beacon, drawing you closer.

If you choose, you can surrender to the Holy Feeling and allow your awareness to flow deeply into it. As you do so, you'll notice the Holy Feeling intensify and start to fill you up and feel bigger, more alive. Continuing to move more deeply into the Holy Feeling with your awareness, at some point, you'll notice a shift. Again, it's not easy to describe, but it will be as if you have moved inside this Holy Feeling. At this point, it's not uncommon to need another period of adjustment from experiencing this feeling as if it had been inside of you to experiencing it as if you are now inside of it.

Linger here for a few more moments. Then begin to bring your awareness to your breathing. Allow your breath to reconnect with your body. Slowly open your eyes.

Each time we move into the heart space in this way and to this degree during our periods of waiting in centering prayer, we make ready the experience of an unquenchable relationship with God.

CENTERING PRAYER

1	**SIT AND CLOSE YOUR EYES** In a quiet and calm space, sit and get comfortable. Then close your eyes.
2	**SETTLE INTO YOUR BODY** Take a few deep breaths through your nose as you become aware of your body.
3	**REPEAT THE PSALM'S FIFTH AND SIXTH LINES** Recall the fifth and sixth lines of Psalm 62: *How long will you assail....* Slowly say each word. Linger on those words that you feel drawn to linger on.
4	**EXPERIENCE YOUR THOUGHTS** As you experience thoughts, notice your body. Become aware of the relationship between sensations in your body and your thoughts.
5	**REST IN YOUR HEART SPACE** Gently move your awareness to your heart space. Become aware of how your waiting feels. As thoughts show up, notice them. Then return to your waiting.
6	**SLOWLY OPEN YOUR EYES** As your centering prayer session comes to a close, bring your awareness to your breath, then to the whole of your body. After a few breaths, slowly open your eyes.

12

How Long Will You Assail to Crush Me

WITH VERSE 3, WE move into the second dynamic of Psalm 62. In looking at the entirety of the verse (*How long will you assail to crush me, all of you together, as if you were a leaning fence, a toppling wall?*), we discover that the psalmist turns his attention towards those who are assailing or attacking him.

In the spirit of reading this psalm through the lens of poetry and symbolism, we can easily expand the focus of the psalmist's words, and give him space actually to personify his thoughts. Now, we understand that he is speaking to the thoughts that invade not just his mind but ours, too. This approach reveals an entirely new layer of meaning and transforms the verse into an illuminating instruction for centering prayer.

How Long?

These thoughts have become mighty and burdensome, seemingly joining forces to destroy the psalmist. The experience has become exhausting and overwhelming. The intensity builds to the point that the thoughts themselves are crushing the psalmist—a feeling that most all of us have experienced at some point. This leads to the well-warranted question that is verse 3, which is essentially *How long will all this continue?*

We'll look at the answer to that question later. However, as a little teaser, the answer rests largely in the hands of the psalmist. Of course, we're invited to ask ourselves the same question. When we do, we'll find that the answer will largely rest in our hands, too. That is good news.

Will You (a.k.a. Your Thoughts)

One of the most paradoxical things about thoughts is that we can't touch, smell, taste, hear, or see them with our physical senses. They have no material reality, yet they have power to drastically affect our material reality as they swirl around our mind, often getting in the way of the experience of our heart. Of course, to be more accurate, we give these thoughts their power, though when we feel the way the psalmist feels at this moment in verse 3, it certainly doesn't seem like we empower these crushing thoughts.

We can categorize each thought by the type of emotion or feeling that fuels it. Some examples of such categories for the heavier thoughts that the psalmist alerts us to include despair, worry, anger, fear, anxiety, stress, loneliness, and overwhelm from the world.

We've all been where the psalmist is as he launches into verse 3. We know how these types of thoughts can be relentless in their attack on us and how destructive that attack can be. As we move forward, let's remember that thoughts have their genesis in the mind, and it's fertile terrain, especially for destructive thoughts like the ones that the psalmist speaks about. Of course, it's also fertile terrain for healthy thoughts. We often forget that.

We're going to spend time in the next chapters to listen carefully to the psalmist expose some of the ways that thoughts gain autonomy, wearing us down, and eventually causing us to choose to move (more) out of alignment with God.

Assail to Crush Me

Isolating this part of the verse (*assail to crush me*) allows us to acknowledge both the power and the experience of being overwhelmed by our thoughts. Just to be clear, this experience can happen outside of centering prayer as well as during it. However, when it happens during our centering prayer time, we have the opportunity to gain relief from these thoughts.

The words *assail* and *crush* work together to paint an extreme picture, one that we can feel in our bones. *To assail* carries the connotation of attacking violently, to afflict in order to create overwhelm, and to criticize with forcefulness. *To crush*, of course, implies to overwhelm with emotional pain, to oppress, as well as to forcefully destroy the structure of something. These very powerful words convey the gravity both of how the situation feels and the actual situation itself.

Body-Mind Connection

To underscore the reality of how thoughts can destabilize us, we need to realize that thoughts do impact the physical body.

As we move through life, we have thousands upon thousands of experiences. For the majority of those events, we have the experience, and we move on. No big deal. However, sometimes we have experiences that we end up clinging to. These experiences eventually settle into different parts of our body, flowing into its very cells. Then due to the body-mind connection, when we think about that experience (usually an unpleasant experience) or its memory is triggered due to an external event, we may feel it and relive it in our body in addition to replaying it in our mind. A classic and serious example is post-traumatic stress disorder (PTSD).

With this knowledge of how thoughts impact both body and mind, we can more fully understand how thoughts can actually cause us to feel as if we are being crushed both in our mind as well as in our body.

...a Leaning Fence, a Toppling Wall

The second part of this verse rounds out the *How long* question by likening the effect of the weight and force of these thoughts to the leaning of a fence or the toppling of a wall. If we look in the gospel of Matthew at the account of Peter's experience of failing to walk on water due to his *little faith*, we'll find an interesting parallel that can amplify this aspect of the instruction.

Let's begin by drawing a parallel between the leaning fence and toppling wall from this psalm with Peter's little faith in the moment he starts to sink into the sea. For indeed, the leaning fence and the toppling wall reference our faith. The combined assault of our thoughts push against our faith until, like a weight pushing against a fence or a wall, it topples our faith like it would topple a wall.

Looking at the Koine Greek in which Matthew's gospel has been written, we can see that Peter's *little faith* is more akin to *single-sided faith* (Ὀλιγόπιστε). The image this evokes is that of a wall. The contrasting expression would be *multi-sided*, like that of a polygon or many-sided structure. In fact, our English word *polygon* comes from the Greek, where the prefix *poly-* means "many" and *gon* means "angles."

If we read the account in the gospel closely, we learn that a constellation of thoughts have come together as the force of doubt and has toppled Peter's single-sided faith. The toppling of his faith has immediate results, causing him to start to sink into the sea. The instruction here is that if we have a robust ("many-sided") faith as opposed to little ("single-sided") faith, then thoughts that form doubt will have no impact on our faith or on our relationship with God.

The Answer to the Question

Now, let's return to the particular instruction being offered through this verse in Psalm 62. In this verse, the psalmist gives us instruction about the power of our thoughts and how they can coalesce or come together to create doubt, which eventually pushes against our faith.

It's up to us to determine if we have single-sided faith or many-sided faith at this point. That is the first step to finding the answer to the question posed in this instruction. If we have single-sided faith in God, then we need to acknowledge it and commend ourselves for having the courage to be honest enough to arrive at this awareness. Next, we need to work with this instruction so that our thoughts do not end up creating a force that topples and crushes our faith.

What does it mean to work with the instruction?

Quite simply, we need to continue to show up for centering prayer. It may seem counterintuitive; however, continuing to develop and deepen our relationship with God through centering prayer does strengthen our faith. It may not seem logical or rational, yet prayer has never been about logic or rationality.

Instructions Drawn From the Psalm

• Thoughts, which cannot be examined by any of our physical senses, can have a concrete impact on our day-to-day life.

• Thoughts can impact our body and how we experience life because of the body-mind connection. In other words, what we experience in the mind, we experience in the body and vice-versa.

• Thoughts can assail us both during and apart from our centering prayer sessions. They can topple our faith and destabilize our centering prayer praxis.

Reflect

• Describe how you usually experience thoughts assailing you.

_____

_____

_____

_____

_____

CENTERING PRAYER

1 **SIT AND CLOSE YOUR EYES**
In a quiet and calm space, sit either on the floor, on a cushion, or in a chair. Get comfortable. Close your eyes.

2 **SETTLE INTO YOUR BODY**
Take a few deep breaths through your nose. Allow yourself to become aware of your body as you say to yourself "For God alone my soul in silence waits."

3 **BREATHE INTO YOUR HEART SPACE**
Shift your awareness to your breath. Let your breath be the vehicle that moves your awareness into your heart space.

4 **OPEN YOUR HEART SPACE**
As your awareness moves into your heart space, allow that space to open more and more with each gentle inhalation.

5 **REST IN YOUR HEART SPACE WITH EXPECTATION**
Allow your awareness to expand slightly from your heart space until you notice subtle sensations like butterflies in your stomach. This is your Holy Ground. Rest here in waiting.

6 **SLOWLY OPEN YOUR EYES**
As your centering prayer session comes to a close, bring your awareness to your breath, then to the whole of your body. After a few breaths, slowly open your eyes.

13

THEY SEEK ONLY TO BRING ME DOWN FROM MY PLACE OF HONOR

THE PSALMIST NOW INFORMS us that these thoughts have one mission: to destabilize us and topple us from the "place of honor." Let's consider this place of honor to be our relationship with God as children of God.

To Bring Me Down

In the First Letter of John, we're told that we are children of God *now*. This is our foundational relationship with God. In other words, it is the starting point. Unfortunately, the forces of the world can at times have us thinking the opposite. When that happens, our relationship with God starts to feel shaky and unsure. It's usually a fast moving spiral downward once we start to take what isn't true for actual truth.

Our being brought down by our thoughts can start to feel like an actual fall. It's quite humbling to reflect on how our own experience of feeling like we're falling due to these thoughts can echo the fall of Adam and Eve. These thoughts that the psalmist alerts us to are the kind that came between humanity and God. Imagine how similar our intensifying thoughts of distance and separation from God are to those that drove Adam and Eve into a life outside the Garden of Eden.

If we personify these thoughts and give them agency, we can easily see how it seems like they want to bring us down, how they desire to destabilize our relationship with God.

My Place of Honor

Truth be told, to be children of the creator of the universe is to inhabit a place of honor. Of course, we don't claim this truth out of arrogance. Rather, hearing and living into this truth moves us toward experiences of profound humility and love that deepen the more we reflect on it.

How this looks in all its fullness, as we're told, is still unfolding. However, that unfolding doesn't change the reality of the truth.

What can distort our perception of that reality is exactly what the psalmist speaks about: believing the malicious thoughts that invade and often thrive in our mind.

Instructions Drawn From the Psalm

• We are children of God at this very moment. That is a truth. Its reality equates to the place of honor that the psalmist speaks about.

• Thoughts that swirl around our mind and create doubt about this truth lead to our subjective falling away from the reality of this truth.

• When this happens, we experience a distance and separation from God.

Reflect

• Describe some of the thoughts that you have experienced that destabilize to some degree your belief that you're a child of God.

_____

_____

_____

_____

_____

CENTERING PRAYER

1

SIT AND CLOSE YOUR EYES
In a quiet and calm space, sit and get comfortable.
Then close your eyes.

2

SETTLE INTO YOUR BODY
Take a few deep breaths through your nose as you
become aware of your body.

3

REPEAT THE PSALM'S EIGHTH LINE
Recall the eighth line of Psalm 62: *lies are their chief
delight.* Slowly say each word. Linger on those words
that you feel drawn to linger on.

4

EXPERIENCE YOUR THOUGHTS
As you experience thoughts, notice your body. Become
aware of the relationship between sensations in your
body and your thoughts.

5

REST IN YOUR HEART SPACE
Gently move your awareness to your heart space.
Become aware of how your waiting feels. As thoughts
show up, notice them. Then return to your waiting.

6

SLOWLY OPEN YOUR EYES
As your centering prayer session comes to a close,
bring your awareness to your breath, then to the whole
of your body. After a few breaths, slowly open your
eyes.

14

LIES ARE THEIR CHIEF DELIGHT

THE WORDS FROM THE psalmist in this line underscore the currency that these types of thoughts traffic in as they seek to destabilize our relationship with God.

Logically Speaking About Lies

When we're not in the midst of a mental storm or in the grips of overwhelm from these thoughts, we can easily see the validity of this half verse. Logically and rationally speaking, we get how much of the negative "talk" that these thoughts attack us with amounts to nothing more than lies. While *lies* is a harsh word, it is an accurate word. Lies are told to wound and to destabilize. Lies are destructive weapons that can and will disrupt our relationship with God.

Their Chief Delight

One of the reasons that lies are so destructive is because they can easily be mistaken for truth. That's where their power rests. Because of this, the psalmist warns us in no uncertain terms that we need to be aware that this will be the weapon of choice used by these types of thoughts.

Again, in moments of calm, we know that the many judgmental stories we tell ourselves (or that we listen to from the world) amount to nothing more than lies. These stories come about due to our participation in the dangerous game that these types of thoughts constantly play. In short, if we were not to believe these lies, they would lose their power over us, and the thoughts would be less apt to impact our relationship with God in a negative way.

The irony is this. Despite these stories being made up of lies, we easily believe them and take them for truth. Sometimes, it's almost too easy of an affair for these thoughts as they spin their lies. We give over to them without questioning sometimes, without resistance. That is, perhaps, why lies become the chief delight of these types of thoughts.

Instructions Drawn From the Psalm

• We need to be mindful that the thoughts spoken about in this verse (and dynamic) will bombard us with lies.

• These lies will be convincing and appear as truth.

• If we lose sight of their attack plan, we may easily become co-authors with these thoughts and create stories in our mind fueled by their lies, thus contributing to the destabilization and perhaps toppling of our relationship with God.

Reflect

• Rather than spinning stories from the lies, how might you minimize their effects and disempower the thoughts fueling the lies?

_____

_____

_____

_____

_____

CENTERING PRAYER

1	**SIT AND CLOSE YOUR EYES** In a quiet and calm space, sit and get comfortable. Then close your eyes.
2	**SETTLE INTO YOUR BODY** Take a few deep breaths through your nose as you become aware of your body.
3	**REPEAT THE PSALM'S NINTH AND TENTH LINES** Recall the ninth and tenth lines of Psalm 62: *They bless with their lips....* Slowly say each word. Linger on those words that you feel drawn to linger on.
4	**NOTICE YOUR THOUGHTS AND THE EMOTIONS AND FEELINGS** As you experience thoughts, notice the emotions and feelings fueling them. Become aware of the relationship between thoughts and emotions/feelings.
5	**REST IN YOUR HEART SPACE** Gently move your awareness to your heart space. Become aware of how your waiting feels. As thoughts show up, notice them. Then return to your waiting.
6	**SLOWLY OPEN YOUR EYES** As your centering prayer session comes to a close, bring your awareness to your breath, then to the whole of your body. After a few breaths, slowly open your eyes.

15

THEY BLESS WITH
THEIR LIPS, BUT IN
THEIR HEARTS THEY
CURSE

WE'VE ARRIVED AT THE last verse in this particular dynamic. Before exploring the instruction from this verse, it's a good idea to pause a moment and articulate the motivation, the strategy, and the manner by which this dynamic unfolds.

Verse 3 opens this group of instructions with the psalmist telling us the end game of the thoughts that show up in this dynamic. Their agenda is to topple our faith in God. Destabilizing our centering prayer praxis figures into this because damaging our praxis will damage or lead us to give up on our relationship with God. Next (in verse 4), the psalmist exposes the primary strategy of these thoughts. They will engage in deceit through lies. Finally, with verse 5 (the focus of this chapter), the psalmist alerts us to how these lies will primarily invade. This verse also makes an important connection between these lies and any wound that lives in the heart.

In the words of the psalmist, these lies will "bless with their lips, but in their hearts they curse." On the surface and due to an apparent set of contrasting actions, it appears to be a two-pronged plan of attack. By analogy, certain deceptive people employ a similar tactic when attempting to manipulate others. In fact, one of the expressions in English to describe this type of person and the accompanying blessing-and-cursing set of lies is, appropriately enough, *two faced*.

Of course, for centering prayer, this verse conveys something far richer and quite pivotal for us. Through a careful read of the psalmist's description, we discover practical information about these lies that includes

1. their structure,

2. their actions, and

3. the pathway that they follow.

We will come to learn that not just any thought can sway or topple our faith. Instead, it is the thought that shows up as a lie that will be the most likely to bring down our faith and destabilize our relationship with God.

The Interior Landscape

Before we unpack these points, let's get clear about the two primary "countries" that make up our interior landscape: the mind and the heart.

The mind is the natural environment of discursive or word-based thoughts. For most of us, it's a rich and very active environment. Engaging in almost any contemplative practice will make one very aware of just how active it can be. The words of our thoughts often have sway over how we process our experiences as we go through life and, in turn, the actions we choose as a result.

The mind itself is a neutral environment. By way of contrast, the thoughts that live out their lives in the mind are rarely neutral. In other words, we most often notice something, and then create a thought of judgment about what we notice. That judgment may be positive, negative, or anywhere in between.

The heart (or heart space) is the natural environment of emotions and feelings. It's an environment that is beyond words. The emotions and feelings that manifest in the heart carry much potential to impact and move us in a particular direction. Our experiences of emotions and feelings tend to be more visceral and felt. This is important.

The Anatomy of a Lie

Just as a connection exists between body and mind, one also exists between mind and heart, and in turn, between thoughts and emotions and feelings. Quite simply, emotions and feelings generate, fuel, and color thoughts. For example, when a certain emotion comes into our awareness, a thought usually gets generated in the mind. The thought remains connected to the emotion and receives energy or nourishment from it. This feeling-thought structure is also the basic anatomy of any lie that wields influence over our beliefs and actions. We could liken its structure to a tree with its roots located in the realm of the heart and its trunk, branches, and leaves existing in the environment of the mind.

While the above process outlines a thought being generated from the space of the heart (emotion or feeling), a thought can also sprout in the mind and then grow roots to the heart. Here's an example. Let's say that a person sees a dog and has a neutral thought that simply acknowledges the dog. Often, in this situation, the neutrality of that thought is fleeting because the thought instantaneously seeks nourishment and begins to reach down into the realm of our heart to plug into our emotions and feelings, which fuel the neutral thought. In turn, the emotion or feeling starts to nuance the thought, adding color or quality to it. When this happens, the thought begins to draw in other emotions or feelings, much like a magnet pulling iron filings to itself, and generates an array of similar thoughts. Then all these thoughts get strung together or woven into a story. This process can unfold in the blink of an eye.

Becoming aware of the anatomy of a lie points to two important facts: a lie inhabits both the world of the mind and the heart, and it draws power from our emotions and feelings to wield influence over our beliefs and actions.

The Action of a Lie

The instruction provided to us in verse 5 is a tour de force that makes known the action of these interior lies. To better appreciate the psalmist's keen insight, it helps to rewrite the verse using specific synonyms in place of the verbs *bless* and *curse*.

> *They make true and justify with their lips,*
> *but in their [our] hearts they inflict suffering.*

Now, the dangerous action that these lies bring into play becomes crystal clear. We should also note that the action continuously flows between the two environments of the interior landscape (mind and heart), manifesting differently in each, while remaining an undivided, potent force.

Here's an example. Starting in the heart, we tap into a feeling of being unloved by God. The feeling is rooted in the heart and inflicts us with suffering and pain at the heart level. Then impulses move up the roots of that feeling, out of the heart and into the mind. Here they manifest the feeling as a thought. In the realm of the mind, the thought gets expressed as words, and the words justify and make the lie seem like truth. In this example, the feelings of not being loved by God and the pain that accompanies those feelings will form a thought that may sound like "I am not worthy of love" or "I am not worth being loved." This thought justifies and seems to make true the lie which we feel in our heart. Due to the body-mind connection, this lie also reverberates throughout the body, saturating and infecting its cells.

The Pathway of a Lie

To understand and appreciate the value of the pathway of a lie, we need to underscore that the actions of a lie, in this context, are directly related to our heart wounds. In other words, we need to de-villainize the lie as much as we can, without minimizing the pain it inflicts.

Because our religion and God wounds live in our hearts, the emotions and feelings that flow from these unhealed wounds cry out in expression of that woundedness. It's not that they are wicked nor the lies that they feed. Rather it's that the emotions and feelings have become skewed in what they express due to the wounds in our heart. These wounded emotions and feelings then fuel thoughts in our mind that influence us to act in ways that minimize or consciously try to efface the pain.

This connection between the wounds in our heart and the thoughts in our mind and the actions that we take create a critical pathway. While it is vital to the maintenance of the lies and thoughts that we listen to and that we become aware of during centering prayer, it is also just as vital to the healing of the wounds in our heart and the restoration of our subjective relationship with God.

With that understanding, we are set to embrace and make wide this natural pathway because it is the same pathway that the Holy Spirit makes use of to heal our wounds during centering prayer.

Honoring the Psalmist's Instructions

Why is this instruction of particular importance for our centering prayer? Quite simply, it can help us better understand why thoughts may be difficult to release, why they feel so powerful and so destructive, and why they may "shake us," to use the words of the psalmist.

One way to honor and work with the psalmist's instructions associated with this verse is to spend time reflecting on how we can find tenderness and compassion for ourselves as we journey into the landscape of our heart and into the healing of our wounds.

Becoming Familiar With Emotions and Feelings

For most of us, the realm of the mind and its discursive thoughts is familiar territory. On the other hand, being aware of emotions and feelings without the discursive thoughts that they fuel may feel like a new world, even a bit foreign and strange.

To gain familiarity, it can be helpful to spend some time working with the following body-based activities. As you work with each, you'll gain awareness around verse 5's instruction as well as insight into its importance while becoming familiar with the path that leads from thoughts to emotions and feelings.

As with the other body-based experiences presented earlier in the book, you may want to read through the steps several times to familiarize yourself with the activities so that you can move through each with your eyes closed.

To begin, take a moment to explore the following question.

What stands out for you as you check in with your thoughts?

_____

_____

_____

_____

_____

Being With Love

Step 1: Close your eyes and take a few breaths as you move your awareness into your mind.

Step 2: Think of a thought about love; notice the words that are attached to the thought.

Step 3: Release the words and notice the emotion/feeling of love that fuels the thought.

Step 4: Allow the emotion/feeling to grow.

Step 5: Follow the emotion/feeling into your heart and rest there for several breaths.

Step 6: Let the emotion/feeling expand into the cells of your body. Become aware of any sensations in your body as you allow the emotion/feeling to settle there.

Step 7: Bring your awareness to your breath as you slowly open your eyes.

After you've completed the first experience, describe what stands out for you.

_____

_____

_____

_____

_____

Being With Frustration

Step 1: Close your eyes and take a few breaths as you move your awareness into your mind.

Step 2: Think of something that recently frustrated you.

Step 3: Notice the words that you attach to one of the thoughts.

Step 4: Release the words and notice the emotion/feeling of frustration that fuels the thought.

Step 5: Allow the emotion/feeling to grow.

Step 6: Let the emotion/feeling expand into the cells of your body. Become aware of any sensations in your body as the emotion/ feeling settles into your body.

Step 7: Bring your awareness to your breath as you release the sensations and the emotions/feelings.

Step 8: Slowly open your eyes.

What stands out for you now after completing this second experience?

_____

_____

_____

_____

Being With Compassion

Step 1: Close your eyes and take a few breaths as you move your awareness into your mind.

Step 2: Think a thought about compassion. Notice the words you attach to the thought.

Step 3: Release the words and notice the emotion/feeling of compassion that fuels the thought.

Step 4: Allow the emotion/feeling to grow.

Step 5: Follow the emotion/feeling into your heart and rest there for several breaths.

Step 6: Let the emotion/feeling expand into the cells of your body. Become aware of any sensations in your body as you allow the emotion/feeling to settle there.

Step 7: Bring your awareness to your breath as you slowly open your eyes.

Describe what stands out for you after this third experience.

_____

_____

_____

_____

_____

Instructions Drawn From the Psalm

• The interior landscape is made up of the mind and the heart. The mind is the realm of discursive thoughts. The heart is the realm of non-discursive emotions and feelings.

• A lie has a feeling-thought structure. It is similar to a tree. The roots are the feelings and emotions located in the heart. The trunk, branches, and leaves are the discursive thoughts found in the mind.

• The discursive thought part of a lie makes us think that the lie is true. The non-discursive part of the lie continuously inflicts our wounded heart with pain and suffering.

• Lies that have the power to influence our actions may unseat our centering prayer praxis and topple our faith in God. These lies are fueled by emotions and feelings.

• The pathway from heart to mind is both the pathway of lies and the pathway the Holy Spirit uses to heal our religion and God wounds.

Reflection

• What are some lies you tell yourself about God / religion / your relationship with God?

_____

_____

_____

_____

_____

• Describe the emotions or feelings that are connected to one of these lies.

_____

_____

_____

_____

• What would it look like for you to embrace these lies with compassion and understanding?

_____

_____

_____

_____

CENTERING PRAYER

1

SIT AND CLOSE YOUR EYES

In a quiet and calm space, sit either on the floor, on a cushion, or in a chair. Get comfortable. Close your eyes.

2

SETTLE INTO YOUR BODY

Take a few deep breaths through your nose. Allow yourself to become aware of your body as you say to yourself "For God alone my soul in silence waits."

3

BREATHE INTO YOUR HEART SPACE

Shift your awareness to your breath. Let your breath be the vehicle that moves your awareness into your heart space.

4

REST IN YOUR HEART SPACE

Allow your awareness to expand slightly from your heart space until you notice subtle sensations like butterflies in your stomach. This is your Holy Ground. Rest here in waiting.

5

NOTICE AND OFFER YOUR THOUGHTS

As you notice thoughts that the Holy Spirit brings into your awareness, release and offer them back to the Holy Spirit. Then return to your Holy Ground and waiting.

6

SLOWLY OPEN YOUR EYES

As your centering prayer session comes to a close, bring your awareness to your breath, then to the whole of your body. After a few breaths, slowly open your eyes.

16

⸻⸻

CHECKING IN AGAIN

THE CHAPTERS FOLLOWING THE last *Check In* have focused on thoughts that we may encounter during our centering prayer praxis. As a whole, these chapters examined the second dynamic of centering prayer. Let's spend a little time exploring what our role is as we experience this thought-laden dynamic.

Life in General

As we move into this exploration, we need to acknowledge that we can experience these types of thoughts both in our everyday life as well as during our periods of centering prayer. However, during centering prayer, we have opportunities to work with these thoughts so that they don't become or remain impediments to our relationship with God. That's big.

Engaging With This Dynamic

The instructions giving us guidance for this dynamic of centering prayer reveal a process that leads us into experiences which deepen our relationship with God. During this process, we consciously choose to open ourselves to God's healing grace. With the help of the Holy Spirit, we clear out the clutter and pain and wounds that live in our heart space, allowing us to experience relationship with God in its fullness.

At the Surface and Below

As we settle into any given centering prayer session, we may notice that thoughts start to crowd our mind, start to interrupt the silence. This can lead us to distraction from our waiting for God. It's actually quite common and is something that will undoubtedly happen in almost each centering prayer experience we undertake.

To keep things in perspective, it's helpful to remember that thoughts and any moments of distraction caused by thoughts actually make up a natural part of centering prayer and, if anything, their presence means that we're engaging in centering prayer as we should be.

The vast majority of these thoughts will fall into the category of the mundane. For example: thoughts about errands or tasks we need to do like going to the grocery store or preparing the next meal or some activity for work. The other category of thoughts that we may encounter will contain thoughts that focus more on our personal life and relationships. These thoughts may focus on pains, regrets, or hurtful experiences. Alternatively, they may be associated with joyful aspects of our life and relationships.

It's important to know that either category of thought may take us away from our waiting for God. From that perspective, we need to give equal weight to all thoughts and handle each of them in the same manner, which we'll turn to shortly.

Reaction and Burying

As the psalmist has made known to us in the previous verses, one of the tendencies we have is to react to our thoughts. That means that we draw conclusions before we take time for honest reflection and discernment. Reaction is usually rash and not based on truth. It can also lead to pain and suffering, ultimately getting in the way of our relationship with God.

One specific type of reaction is the burying of these thoughts. For whatever reason, it feels like the right and the safest thing we can do when we're being bombarded by them. Despite it feeling like a good thing or even the only thing that we can do, rest assured that it isn't. Therefore, to be clear, we don't want to bury or suppress our thoughts. When we choose to, we set ourselves up for future pain because somehow or some way these thoughts will resurface. When they do, they're usually more volatile and carry with them more potential to disrupt and destabilize our life and our relationship with God.

The Holy Spirit Offers

If we agree that neither reacting to nor burying our unhealthy thoughts is what we want to do, we need to understand how to handle such thoughts in a supportive way. How would that actually look?

This is where we want to bring the Holy Spirit back into our exploration. Let's remember that the Holy Spirit lives in our heart space. Because of this truth, we need to acknowledge that the Holy Spirit knows and understands each of our hearts in a very intimate way. The Holy Spirit is more familiar with our hearts, the very depth of our hearts, than we ourselves are. That being the case, the Holy Spirit knows exactly what has been stored in each of our hearts that is getting in the way of our relationship with God. The Holy Spirit knows all that we're holding on to that we would do well to release to begin healing.

Now, we are set to see these distracting and destructive thoughts appearing in the mind during centering prayer in a completely new way. We're ready to see that the Holy Spirit brings these thoughts to us, to our consciousness. This is why they're showing up during centering prayer. Not only does the Holy Spirit bring these thoughts into our awareness, but the Holy Spirit offers them to us.

In offering each thought to us, we're offered two choices. We can choose to hold on to the thought; or we can choose to release, surrender, and return it to the Holy Spirit.

It doesn't matter the content of the thought. It can be mundane or grave. If the Holy Spirit brings it into our awareness, then it's a thought that occupies our heart space in some manner. It's not necessary for us to figure out why. It's only necessary for us to choose what to do: hold on to it or surrender it.

If we hold on to it, we may start to fixate on it during our centering prayer. We may start to be drawn into its story. Alternatively, we may try to push it back down, bury it, suppress it from our awareness, sweeping it under the rug, so to speak.

If we surrender and offer it back to the Holy Spirit, we're unburdened and can return to our waiting for God.

Sin and Forgiveness

Let's bring sin and forgiveness back into the conversation. They both factor into how we show up during this dynamic of our centering prayer.

Earlier in the book, we reframed the definition of sin so that we move away from reaction and move toward honesty and acceptance. We defined sin as anything that moves us out of alignment or harmony with God. The impact of that misalignment or disharmony is a weakening of our relationship with God.

125

According to Origen of Alexandria, sin distorts, obscures, or erodes our relationship with God. Salvation restores it. Origen reminds us that sin leads to an estrangement or alienation from God on our part.

Of course, theologians and Tradition use different words, come from different starting places, and add other criteria to determine what sin is. While not unimportant, all these other aspects of sin can cause us to lose sight of how disruptive our thoughts can be and how they have the potential to move us out of relationship with God, even to the point of destabilizing our relationship with God. In this way, we can identify and label certain thoughts (and, in turn, actions) as sin.

Forgiveness is an action that restores us from sin. It's an action that brings us back into alignment and harmony with God.

In the pages of this book, we're surely not pretending to explore the richness and depth of all that is implied by the concept of *forgiveness*. However, in relation to how we can deepen our relationship with God through centering prayer, let's at least start to unpack this powerful and essential act we call *forgiveness*.

In Colossians 3:13, we are instructed that we "must forgive." Some may read that verse and interpret it as a finger-wagging, forceful decree, and then shut down around it and simply dismiss it. Instead, how would it be to receive the instruction in a different way? How would it be to hear a softer, more intimate, even vulnerable and caring voice speaking so as to draw us onto the path to a deep and profound relationship with God? Take a moment to hear those words from Colossians not as a hard-edged command but as a welcoming and liberating invitation. Let that tone influence your relationship with forgiveness. Then take that with you into each centering prayer session.

Releasing as Our Part in Forgiveness

Sometimes we can be so familiar with a word that we start to lose understanding about its meaning in a deep, specific, and precise sense. That can be said about the word *forgiveness*.

One of the primary meanings of *forgiveness* is "a release." When we forgive someone, we release them, or more specifically, we release the hurt they have caused us. When we hold onto and store in our body and mind some hurt or pain caused by an event or someone in our life, then that becomes an impediment to love. It gets in the way of our being able to receive and to give love. This can acutely show up during centering prayer. If we enter into centering prayer with the intention and expectation of deepening our relationship with God, we must do our part to remove these impediments to love.

This is where the Holy Spirit comes into play. If the Holy Spirit offers us those thoughts and emotions that get in the way of love, then it's our job to release our attachment to them. It's our job to surrender them and hand them over to the Holy Spirit. As we do this, the Holy Spirit lovingly accepts our offering as a type of holy sacrifice. Through the Holy Spirit, these thoughts and emotions move into the presence of God. As that happens, they lose their power (over us) and dissolve because no sin, nothing that is out of alignment and harmony with the love of God, can exist in God.

Kenosis

Kenosis is one of those terms that can often feel like some kind of secret code, often spoken with great fluency in certain Christian circles. It comes to us from Greek and means "an emptying." That's straightforward enough; however, because of the richness and nuances of meaning that can be communicated by *kenosis*, it may be somewhat difficult at times to understand what is being conveyed or how it applies to a particular topic.

According to many wise Christian teachers today, like Richard Rohr and Cynthia Bourgeault, several key events of kenosis have taken place. The first such event was when God emptied God's self to create this universe. The next major event of kenosis was when God emptied God's self to become human. The Holy Trinity illustrates the eternality of kenosis, and becomes a sort of icon or template that leads us to a more nuanced and even personal meaning of kenosis as "self-emptying."

When kenosis applies to God, it's a self-emptying of divinity. For us, it's more about a self-emptying of those parts of our humanity that get in the way of our relationship with God.

Our kenosis, in part, is about emptying ourselves of sin. Sin is part of the human condition. (Because that last sentence can feel like a type of judgment or an example of potential weaponization, read it spaciously.) Like it or not, we tend to get attached and give our power to those thoughts and actions that move us out of alignment and harmony with God.

So how does our kenosis actually look in centering prayer? It looks like forgiveness. We give over (release) our attachment to thoughts and actions that get in the way of our intimate relationship with God. For example, we let go of and empty ourselves of harmful thoughts, past wounds, and unhealthy choices that lead to unhealthy actions. Through forgiveness we're invited to release each.

Remember that Paul counseled us to do this (to forgive) in Colossians 3:13. Each time we forgive, we create more space in our heart, more opportunity for deep relationship and union with God. Here we're once again on Holy Ground with our centering prayer.

Key Points

• During centering prayer, the Holy Spirit presents us with our thoughts and emotions and feelings.

• The thoughts, emotions, and feelings that the Holy Spirit reveals to us are actually getting in the way of our relationship with God. They are keeping us out of alignment and harmony with God. We have the choice to offer them back to the Holy Spirit or to hold on to them.

• Offering back these thoughts and emotions and feelings to the Holy Spirit is a type of forgiveness or kenosis, which leads to a healing and cleansing of our heart.

• Forgiveness restores our alignment and harmony with God.

• We tenderly approach this Holy Ground of forgiveness as we enter into centering prayer.

Reflection

• Describe how knowing that thoughts, emotions, and feelings flow into your mind during centering prayer due to the action of the Holy Spirit affects your relationship with them.

_____

_____

_____

_____

_____

_____

_____

_____

• How does this understanding shift your relationship with your centering prayer praxis?

_____

_____

_____

_____

CENTERING PRAYER

1	**SIT AND CLOSE YOUR EYES** In a quiet and calm space, sit and get comfortable. Then close your eyes.
2	**SETTLE INTO YOUR BODY** Take a few deep breaths through your nose as you become aware of your body.
3	**REST IN YOUR HEART SPACE** Gently move your awareness to your heart space. Become aware of how your waiting feels.
4	**NOTICE AND OFFER YOUR THOUGHTS** As you notice thoughts that the Holy Spirit brings into your awareness, release and offer them back to the Holy Spirit. Then return to your Holy Ground.
5	**EXPLORE** Once again in the Holy Ground of your heart, be present to how it is different this time. Notice all that comes into your awareness.
6	**SLOWLY OPEN YOUR EYES** As your centering prayer session comes to a close, bring your awareness to your breath, then to the whole of your body. After a few breaths, slowly open your eyes.

17

❦

FOR GOD ALONE
MY SOUL IN SILENCE
WAITS

AFTER HAVING RECEIVED INSTRUCTION focused on thoughts that get brought into our awareness by the Holy Spirit, we find ourselves being ushered into the next dynamic of centering prayer with the same words that began the psalm: *For God alone my soul in silence waits.* Two main characteristics of the instructions within this new dynamic include word repetition and subtle shifts in language. Both enrich the instructions and our understanding.

The bookend or bracketing feature provided by the repetition of this half verse signals a primary movement of centering prayer: a return again and again to the silence and the waiting. We begin by sitting with our eyes closed and settling into the silence as we wait for God (or more aptly as we wait for our awareness to notice God). Then thoughts and internal chatter start to arise. Eventually they not only invade the silence but easily proliferate and end up cluttering our minds to the point that we no longer find ourselves in silence. These thoughts may even cause us to become overwhelmed ("shaken"). However, as we offer them over and release them to the Holy Spirit, we find ourselves back in the silence and waiting for God.

The Same Yet Different

When reading through the other verses that make up this particular dynamic, we see that the psalmist doesn't present us with a word-for-word repetition of previous verses. That fact is worth noting because it implies a progression. It implies that our experience at this point won't be exactly the same as when we first entered our centering prayer. The differences may be small, but let's not equate that fact to being insignificant.

This repetition effectively starts to serve, in part, as a yield sign, suggesting that we pause to consider our internal surroundings at those moments following each return to silence and waiting. As we bring our awareness to these moments, we notice that each is different. We find ourselves back in the silence, but the silence is different. We're in the midst of the waiting again, but the waiting is different.

Silence

As we return to the silence, after having offered over what the Holy Spirit has presented to us, we are, in essence, offering our consent to God. This release and return infuses the silence with a spacious quality. This spaciousness serves to open our contracted (even overwhelmed) minds and to open our hearts, making them less hardened and more transparent and tender.

To make sense of the rich meaning conveyed in the word *silence*, let's focus on one characteristic of centering prayer: non-discursiveness. That means that this type of prayer doesn't use words. Essentially, it's beyond words, and that's significant.

We're using centering prayer to move into the heart, which is a reality beyond words. However, the mind is an experience of thoughts, and thoughts exist through words. If we use words or get drawn into the stories of our thoughts during centering prayer, we'll tend to stay in the mind, and it becomes much more challenging to move into the experience of our heart.

For a poignant example of this, we only need to look at John 20:14-16. The few verses before this section reveal Mary standing before the tomb of Jesus telling two angels why she is weeping. She's spinning in her mind, trying to get information about where Jesus's body has disappeared to. Then in verse 14 Mary turns around and sees Jesus but doesn't recognize him. When Jesus asks her why she's weeping, she answers him from the place of her mind, from the place of trying to discover and resolve the mystery of what has happened to Jesus's body. Swirling in that mind space, she answers Jesus with the particulars about the situation of the missing body.

There's a lesson for us here. Even when the risen Lord asks us a question with the intention of taking us to our heart and to a deeper relationship with him, our usual and initial go-to response is from the mind and some story that lives there. Asking a question such as why Mary is weeping begs a response from the heart. Yet, as we see, Mary gets pulled into her swirling thoughts to the point that she even turns away from Jesus as she's talking. Perhaps she turns to look at the empty tomb, still trying to make sense of things. But the point is, she turns away from Jesus and from the space of her heart and the Lord of her heart.

To help her get into her heart and into the presence of real relationship with him in that very moment, Jesus calls her name. That does it! Mary turns back to look at Jesus, signaling her shift into her heart. Her heart recognizes her teacher and risen Lord when her eyes cannot, when her mind cannot. It's striking, and it's a good example of what God is doing with us in the silence of centering prayer through the Holy Spirit, particularly when we get overwhelmed and even trapped by our thoughts.

Simply put, our thoughts tend to be discursive. We generally speak words to ourselves when thinking or ruminating over our thoughts or when using them to tell ourselves stories from our past or about our future. Alternatively, we can cultivate silence and move into our heart space as we release internal dialogue and thoughts to the Holy Spirit.

The Quality of Silence

Merely thinking about silence can be a frightening experience for some of us. Images of emptiness and desolation can quickly populate our mind. To be clear, the silence of centering prayer doesn't possess those qualities. It's not empty or sterile or desolate. Rather, this silence brims with a certain fullness of potentiality that deepens and even becomes fuller as we give over and consent to our relationship with God.

The silence of centering prayer is a satisfying experience and can be likened to a landscape where nothing good and beautiful is lacking. It's an experience that can move us beyond material thoughts, opening our awareness to a reality outside of time and in which we may indeed have robust experiences of the heart by using the senses of our heart.

Benedict of Nursia (St. Benedict), lived in the late 5th and early 6th centuries and was the founder of western monasticism. He wrote a rule of life, now known as *The Rule of St. Benedict*, for monastics to order their daily lives around work and prayer. In his Rule, St. Benedict makes reference to these senses of the heart, or at least one of the senses (listening/hearing). Specifically, in the Prologue of his Rule, he invites each of us to "listen with the ear of your heart." Recalling the Gospel passage from John, we can witness another example of these senses when

Mary turns to Jesus for the second time. The eyes and ears of Mary's heart are the senses that responded to Jesus. They're the senses that recognized Jesus. They're the senses that opened her awareness to the experience of a new and life-changing reality.

Waiting

Some verbs, at times, describe a middle ground. They're not active; they don't describe an action like *run* or *sit*. Also, they're not passive; they don't receive or have action done to them. Instead, this particular class of verbs conveys a state of being. The verb *wait* falls into this category as it is used in Psalm 62.

It asks us to begin to sense the waiting as a space or a container in which our centering prayer unfolds. It's more than simple passiveness. However, it's not an act of force or will power, as in trying to create a forcefield to keep out thoughts and words. Instead, this *waiting* is a space in which we remain attentive, in which we notice and experience. It's a space in which we find ourselves inhabiting our heart. It's in the waiting where we encounter God.

So let's check in with the quality of our waiting in centering prayer. Let's give over to God and allow our waiting to be an openness and a surrender, so we can receive what God wants to be and to express to us in the moment. This waiting gives space to God. The Holy Spirit of God brings life to us and vivifies our relationship in the waiting. Let's be open to receiving life and relationship in all its fullness.

Instructions Drawn From the Psalm

• The verses of this dynamic offer instruction through the use of repetition, revealing subtler aspects of centering prayer.

• The silence of centering prayer is not sterile or empty; it is imbued with a fullness of experience beyond the words of our thoughts and stories.

• Waiting within centering prayer is neither passive nor active. It's a holding of space (a surrender and a consent) in our heart so that we can be more fully with God.

Reflect

• How do the repetition of words and subtle changes in phrasing within the lines of this dynamic speak to you?

_____

_____

_____

_____

_____

CENTERING PRAYER

1   **SIT AND CLOSE YOUR EYES**
In a quiet and calm space, sit either on the floor, on a cushion, or in a chair. Get comfortable. Close your eyes.

2   **SETTLE INTO YOUR BODY**
Take a few deep breaths through your nose. Allow yourself to become aware of your body as you say to yourself "For God alone my soul in silence waits."

3   **BREATHE INTO YOUR HEART SPACE**
Shift your awareness to your breath. Let your breath be the vehicle that moves your awareness into your heart space.

4   **REST IN YOUR HEART SPACE**
Allow your awareness to expand slightly from your heart space until you notice subtle sensations like butterflies in your stomach. This is your Holy Ground. Rest here in waiting.

5   **NOTICE AND OFFER YOUR THOUGHTS**
As you notice thoughts that the Holy Spirit brings into your awareness, release and offer them back to the Holy Spirit. Then return to your Holy Ground and waiting.

6   **SLOWLY OPEN YOUR EYES**
As your centering prayer session comes to a close, bring your awareness to your breath, then to the whole of your body. After a few breaths, slowly open your eyes.

18

TRULY, MY HOPE IS
IN HIM

IN MY EARLIER LIFE, hope was an experience that was often elusive. Perhaps it was because I didn't understand what hope actually is, and so I didn't know when I was truly experiencing hope. Of course, part of the confusion came about because I often conflated hope with faith. The two seemed so similar in my mind, with only a hair's breadth of difference between them, if even that much. Yet, as I've come to learn, a substantial difference exists between faith and hope; and it's relevant.

Faith is the belief that something is true, despite any lack of first-hand experience of the fact. As such, faith is actually a precursor to hope, and without faith, hope can't exist. The half verse discussed in this chapter points us to this fact and helps us see the necessity of hope in relation to deepening our relationship with God through centering prayer.

Truly

This half verse starts with the word *truly*. This little word serves as a signpost for us announcing that the type of hope that the psalmist is extolling is not a half-hearted wish. It's not in the same category as that expressed in a greeting card. Rather, the word *truly* leads us to understand that the psalmist speaks with certitude and conviction. These qualities amplify, underscore, and qualify the type of hope that leads us to God. It's a hope that's imbued with faith, leaving no room for doubt.

My Hope Is in Him

When we wait in centering prayer in the manner that the psalmist has instructed, we're bearing witness to a hope not in something ordinary or mundane, but a hope in God. That can be overwhelming to think about, something even beyond our ability to fully comprehend. However, because we have been told much about God in the previous verses, we can allow the essence of this particular hope, its sureness and security, to unfold and fill the heart.

Let's look at what this means for our centering prayer. Hope serves our centering prayer praxis by rightly orienting us toward God from the very beginning. It's our hope, even if not consciously apparent, that actually moves us to choose for centering prayer, to sit down, and to enter into that silence where we can wait with a certainty beyond expectation that God will show up, that our waiting will not be in vain. Through that hope, we find ourselves experiencing a peace of mind that gives rise to anticipation.

This anticipation, if we examine it closely, is not a mental, agitated anticipation, which would carry with it thoughts of anxiousness and nervousness. Rather, this anticipation has a spaciousness to it that allows and invites us to settle more deeply into our heart.

Parallel Verses

The psalmist brings out another aspect of hope, one that is perhaps subtler and requires us to piece together two half verses to bring it to light. It's worth the effort, however, because it can help us link hope to one of the purposes for centering prayer.

To begin, let's look at what happens when we align verse 1b with this current half verse (6b).

(1b) *From him comes my salvation,*
(6b) *Truly, my hope is in him.*

As we recall that *salvation* means the restoration of our relationship with God, we also recall that the act of that restoration comes from God. He restores the relationship. Of course, according to the New Testament scriptures, this restoration has already taken place, despite perhaps life not matching our idea of what that salvation should look like on a personal level.

Ontologically and objectively, our relationship with God has been restored. However, most of us don't get this in a subjective, real, and lived sense. Perhaps we get glimpses of it, but through our centering prayer, we're heading toward those profound and sustained experiences beyond the glimpses. The subjective restoration of our relationship with God is what our centering prayer praxis can effect.

Through these two half verses, we are reminded that our post-resurrection hope *is* in God's ongoing project of restoring a *subjective* experience of the ontological reality of our already-restored relationship with him. You may need to read that last sentence twice, but it's worth it.

Instructions Drawn From the Psalm

• Our hope rests on our faith. It's linked to a lived, subjective experience of our restored relationship with God.

• One of the reasons for a centering prayer praxis is to move closer to a sustained, subjective experience of our reconciled relationship with God.

Reflect

• Describe the ways in which you experience a disconnect between the ontological reality of your salvation and your subjective experience of it.

_____

_____

_____

_____

_____

_____

_____

_____

• What speaks to you from this half verse? How can it support your centering prayer?

_____

_____

_____

_____

_____

CENTERING PRAYER

1   **SIT AND CLOSE YOUR EYES**
In a quiet and calm space, sit and get comfortable. Then close your eyes.

2   **SETTLE INTO YOUR BODY**
Take a few deep breaths through your nose as you become aware of your body.

3   **REPEAT THE PSALM'S THIRTEENTH AND FOURTEENTH LINES**
Recall the thirteenth and fourteenth lines of Psalm 62: *He alone is my rock....* Slowly say each word. Linger on those words that you feel drawn to linger on.

4   **EXPERIENCE THE PROTECTION OF GOD**
Notice your body. Become aware of sensations of safety and protection from God. Notice how you feel in your body as you stay with these sensations.

5   **REST IN YOUR HEART SPACE WITH EXPECTATION**
Gently move your awareness to your heart area. Become aware of how your waiting feels. Be present to the sensations and to what shows up.

6   **SLOWLY OPEN YOUR EYES**
As your centering prayer session comes to a close, bring your awareness to your breath, then to the whole of your body. After a few breaths, slowly open your eyes.

19

〰️

He Alone Is

We're still in somewhat familiar territory as we move to the next verse of this dynamic. The entire verse reads:

He alone is my rock and my salvation,
my stronghold, so that I shall not be shaken.

This verse first appeared as verse 2. Its repetition is a device that calls our attention to a more nuanced reading of the original instruction.

During its debut as verse 2, we were not told why we needed God to be a stronghold or from what we needed protection in the context of centering prayer. However, at this point in the dynamics of our centering prayer experience, we understand that thoughts can show up, and at times, they can feel unrelenting and overwhelming. It's important to know at both the cellular and heart levels that God provides help and protection from the power that our thoughts wield, even in the midst of their bombardment.

Repetition Calls for Attention

The repetition of this verse honors and validates the lived experience of overwhelm from our thoughts during centering prayer while, at the same time, reminding us that God has our back in the midst of these experiences. Let's pause a moment and let that sink deeply into our heart space.

Reviewing the initial instructions of this dynamic, we understand that after releasing our thoughts into the hands of the Holy Spirit, we're called to bring our awareness back to God (verse 6), who is our rock, salvation, and stronghold (verse 7). It's that simple. Yet, to be honest, returning to the silence (or even finding the silence again) can, at times, be challenging.

Working With the Instruction

The nuanced reading we're invited to apply to this instruction can help us more easily make this return to silence and waiting. This deeper reading centers around the phrases *my rock*, *my salvation*, and *my stronghold*.

The technique of repetition that the psalmist employs begs us to expand and then amplify the connotations of these three phrases. We create a largesse that helps draw us back into the silence as we read *my rock* and hear "the Ground of my Being," as we read *my salvation* and hear "my Savior," and as we read *my stronghold* and hear "my Protector."

Then we can move this nuanced read of the instruction into a bodily sense of God as Ground of Being if we work with this instruction as a separate practice (presented on p. 150).

In working with the following Ground of Being practice, it's good to stay with each step until it feels right to move to the next. It's also good to work with this practice more than once. Each experience will be unique, and you may find yourself lingering longer at different steps each time you engage the practice.

The intention here is to allow God to reveal in an experiential way how it feels in the body to have God as the Ground of your Being and your Protector. Afterward, your cellular memory will help you move more easily into that bodily experience during (and outside of) centering prayer, particularly when you need to start remembering these qualities of God after feelings of being bombarded and overwhelmed by your thoughts.

Experiencing the Ground of Our Being

Step 1 Sit comfortably and close your eyes.

Step 2 Become aware of your breath and use it to settle into your body.

Step 3 Notice where in your body you feel grounded. Allow your awareness to linger in this place.

Step 4 After a few moments, imagine God's presence in this place of groundedness. Let any images or sensations or imaginings of God's presence unfold. Then bring yourself into the scene. Incorporate as many of your senses as you can into this experience.

Step 5 As you feel ready and while still in that space of God's presence, imagine God as your source of protection and safety. Imagine God as your protector. Again, allow the experience to unfold through as many of your senses as you can.

Step 6 When you feel the time is right, let the experience flow into the cells of your body and notice any sensations that move into your awareness.

Step 7 When ready, return your awareness to your breathing and slowly open your eyes.

Instructions Drawn From the Psalm

• This verse is a repetition of an earlier verse and offers an opportunity for a deeper, more nuanced instruction.

• Coming on the heels of the previous dynamic, which focused on being bombarded and overwhelmed by our thoughts, the psalmist uses this verse to remind us that God does indeed offer help and protection from our thoughts and the ensuing overwhelm.

• We can work with this instruction to create experiences and cellular memory of God as the Ground of our Being and Source of Protection.

• If we find coming back to the silence of waiting challenging at any point, we can simply recall from cellular memory the experience of God as our Ground of Being and Source of Protection.

151

Reflect

• Describe how "being shaken" shows up for you.

_____

_____

_____

_____

_____

_____

_____

_____

• Describe how "being shaken" during your centering prayer may serve to help gauge the degree to which you've made God the Ground of your Being.

_____

_____

_____

_____

• What circumstance(s) in centering prayer may lead to being shaken despite having made God the Ground of your Being, your Savior, and your Protector?

_____

_____

_____

_____

_____

_____

_____

_____

CENTERING PRAYER

1

SIT AND CLOSE YOUR EYES
In a quiet and calm space, sit either on the floor, on a cushion, or in a chair. Get comfortable. Close your eyes.

2

SETTLE INTO YOUR BODY
Take a few deep breaths through your nose. Allow yourself to become aware of your body as you say to yourself "For God alone my soul in silence waits."

3

BREATHE INTO YOUR HEART SPACE
Shift your awareness to your breath. Let your breath be the vehicle that moves your awareness into your heart space.

4

REST IN YOUR HEART SPACE
Allow your awareness to expand slightly from your heart space until you notice subtle sensations like butterflies in your stomach. This is your Holy Ground. Rest here in waiting.

5

NOTICE AND OFFER YOUR THOUGHTS
As you notice thoughts that the Holy Spirit brings into your awareness, release and offer them back to the Holy Spirit. Then return to your Holy Ground and waiting.

6

SLOWLY OPEN YOUR EYES
As your centering prayer session comes to a close, bring your awareness to your breath, then to the whole of your body. After a few breaths, slowly open your eyes.

20

IN GOD IS MY SAFETY AND MY HONOR

THIS HALF VERSE HAS a crucial mission. It calls out and endeavors to get our attention and wake us up. Anytime we see a verse starting out with *In God*, we need to pay attention. With the words of this half verse, it's as if the psalmist is crying out to us about the power of God's love, asking us not only to be aware of it but actually to experience it in our being, and in this case, through two specific truths that show up as feelings of safety and honor.

It's a message that can profoundly affect our centering prayer. Regardless of the type and intensity of the thoughts that come into our awareness during centering prayer, invoking these truths can support a confident and sure return to the silence of our waiting. With that in mind, let's unpack this half verse.

In God Is My Safety

Here we find ourselves face-to-face with the words *in God*. It's a phrase, in all honesty, that can bewilder. It can also fall flat with us in the midst of our busy lives, when we have precious little time for pausing and reflecting. To restore life and power to this evocative phrase, let's actually take a moment to pause and call on our imagination while reading the following paragraph. We'll let the images of the scene unfold in the mind's eye, lingering with each sentence so the imagination can bring it to life.

You're standing in the center of a large field bordered by tall trees. The field is blanketed with soft green grass and colorful flowers. A path winds along the tree line, out into the field, and toward you. While looking into the distance, you see God walking along the path toward you. As God passes the flowers and trees that grow near the path, you notice that all their colors grow richer and more vibrant. As God continues to approach, you become aware of a type of aura or forcefield that surrounds God. It's transparent yet luminous. The intensity and vibrance of the colors of everything that comes in proximity to God actually give shape and form to this forcefield. Then God arrives and stands close to you. As you look at God, you notice that you are now inside the forcefield. Being in the presence of God, inside this space, is being in harmony with God. This harmony rarifies everything's beauty and offers unmistakeable and unshakeable safety. It is as if all that passes into God's aura and presence becomes cleansed and transformed, resting in harmony with God. In essence, nothing harmful can pass into God's presence without being transformed and harmonized with God. As you look around from inside this aura of God, you notice that somehow the aura has expanded to the point that it actually has no boundaries. It is limitless. This is the landscape of your heart in which God lives.

It's with these images in mind that this instruction from the psalm comes to life and more fully serves our centering prayer praxis. There's value in spending time with these images in our imagination, invoking as many of our senses as we can and allowing the scene to be felt deeply within the cells of our body, reverberating throughout our being.

And My Honor

The last words of this half verse, *and my honor*, may not be typically associated with centering prayer. However, if we understand these words in relation to God, we can let them help us return to our waiting and to our heart.

Let's begin by looking at *honor*'s Hebrew root (*kabhodh*). Its meaning is linked to a certain weightiness or heaviness that is associated with importance, worth, and value. In English, the expression *to carry weight* conveys a similar concept. For example: *that person's opinion carries weight* is a way of expressing the fact that what that person thinks is important and has value, and we would do well to honor it.

157

Building on this understanding, we can sit with and ponder the reality about which this instruction is reminding us: our importance and worth are grounded *in God*. If we let this instruction settle into the body and mind, we can recall it in an experiential way when we find ourselves bombarded by thoughts that fuel doubt about our value and erode our self-esteem.

This can be useful as we get caught up in the swirl of doubt-forming thoughts that may show up during our centering prayer. If we find ourselves struggling to release them to the Holy Spirit, we can breathe and recall this instruction, feeling it in the body. This experiential remembering during these moments will help us release the thoughts more easily, and return to the silence and waiting.

Instructions Drawn From the Psalm

• When we move to the landscape of our heart, we enter into the presence of God. Here is where we can rest in safety, confident that the troubles caused by our thoughts have no reality.

• Our honor, what gives us worth, flows from being *in God*. This is an eternal truth, a vibrant and robust reality.

Reflect

• What does it feel like in your body and mind when you experience thoughts that attack your safety and honor (e.g., your worth)?

_____

_____

_____

_____

_____

• After working with the visualization activity in this chapter, describe your experience and how it affects your relationship with God.

_____

_____

_____

_____

_____

_____

_____

_____

_____

_____

CENTERING PRAYER

1   **SIT AND CLOSE YOUR EYES**
In a quiet and calm space, sit and get comfortable. Then close your eyes.

2   **SETTLE INTO YOUR BODY**
Take a few deep breaths through your nose as you become aware of your body.

3   **REST IN YOUR HEART SPACE**
Gently move your awareness to your heart space. Become aware of how your waiting feels.

4   **NOTICE AND OFFER YOUR THOUGHTS**
As you notice thoughts that the Holy Spirit brings into your awareness, release and offer them back to the Holy Spirit. Then return to your Holy Ground.

5   **EXPLORE**
Once again in the Holy Ground of your heart, be present to how it is different this time. Notice all that comes into your awareness.

6   **SLOWLY OPEN YOUR EYES**
As your centering prayer session comes to a close, bring your awareness to your breath, then to the whole of your body. After a few breaths, slowly open your eyes.

21

GOD IS MY STRONG ROCK AND MY REFUGE

WITH THE WORDS *GOD is my strong rock and my refuge*, the psalmist invites us into the depth of this current dynamic. It is here that he asks us to pause to receive a subtle instruction.

Through the motif of repetition of verse, along with its accompanying variations, the psalmist discloses the characteristic pattern of repeatedly coming back to the silence. As touched upon when we started exploring this dynamic, the process of coming back again and again allows us to gain "ground," so to speak, in our heart. In other words, in returning to the silence, we don't return to the same exact interior space. To use the analogy of physical distance, we return to a place that is a few feet further inside our hearts. It's similar terrain, but not exactly the same place.

My Strong Rock

Earlier in the psalm, in verse 2, the psalmist described God as *my rock*. Now, he describes God as *my strong rock*, emphasizing a slightly different experience of *rock*. Let's use this instruction about gaining "ground" to work with experiences of frustration that we may encounter when we find ourselves needing to return to the silence again and again. If we use the guidance of this instruction to inform our awareness, we can allow for curiosity to develop (as opposed to frustration) as we become aware that this moment of return has brought us to a different place within the landscape of our heart.

My Refuge

While using this half verse to encourage us to deepen our awareness of God, the psalmist balances the image of God being *my strong rock* with the image of God as *my refuge*.

Refuge is not only a place of safety and security, a type of port in the storm, but it also has a nurturing, soft quality to it. Born out of strength, a refuge protects and also nurtures and comforts, offering sanctuary, peace, and healing.

Crucial to this instruction is how it points to increased intimacy with God each time we return to the silence, each time we move further into the heart, each time we open more fully to healing and relationship with God, who is our strong rock and our refuge.

Instructions Drawn From the Psalm

• Each time we come back to waiting in silence, we come back to an interior space deeper in our heart.

• The deeper we go in our heart, the more intimate our experience with God.

Reflect

• How does the awareness that each return to silence brings you to a different place within your heart and a more intimate experience with God affect you?

_____

_____

_____

_____

_____

CENTERING PRAYER

1	**SIT, CLOSE YOUR EYES, AND SETTLE** In a quiet and calm space, sit and get comfortable. Then close your eyes as you settle into your body.
2	**REPEAT THE PSALM'S SEVENTEENTH AND EIGHTEENTH LINES** Recall the seventeenth and eighteenth lines of Psalm 62: *Put your trust....* Slowly say each word. Linger on those words that you feel drawn to linger on.
3	**NOTICE HOW TRUST IN GOD SHOWS UP IN YOUR BODY** Invite your trust in God into your awareness. Notice how you experience it in your body, your mind, and your heart.
4	**REST IN YOUR HEART SPACE** Gently move your awareness to your heart space. Notice any emotions/feelings the Holy Spirit offers. As you're able, be present to the emotions/feelings.
5	**LET THE EMOTIONS/FEELINGS SUBSIDE AND RELEASE THEM** Allow any emotions/feelings to subside and resolve. Then offer them back to the Holy Spirit. Return to your waiting.
6	**SLOWLY OPEN YOUR EYES** As your centering prayer session comes to a close, bring your awareness to your breath, then to the whole of your body. After a few breaths, slowly open your eyes.

22

PUT YOUR TRUST IN
HIM ALWAYS...

THROUGHOUT THIS DYNAMIC OF centering prayer, the psalmist has spoken to us about moving more deeply into the heart. Now, with this dynamic's final verse and instruction, the psalmist shifts his tone. One can imagine emotion starting to overcome him as he begins to use language of place, almost pleading with us, to draw us into an experience born out of a deeper reality of the heart, of healing, and of a more intimate relationship with God.

Through the words of this verse—*Put your trust in him always, O people, pour out your hearts before him, for God is our refuge*—a clear sense of authority overcomes the reader. It's not a harsh authority by any stretch of the imagination. Rather, we get that the psalmist has lived experience of this place that is

God. He has traveled the path of this dynamic that leads into the very heart of vulnerability, both ours and God's.

Put Your Trust in Him Always, O People

This instruction is imbued with such emotion. Reading these words while imagining the psalmist pleading with us to put our trust in God shifts the tone of the instruction. No longer is this a command, but rather a heartfelt appeal. Up to this point, the psalmist as a wise teacher has been (in part) building a case for why we should put our trust in God. We have learned that God is our rock, our salvation, our stronghold, and our refuge. The psalmist has been revealing that these are actually qualities of God, perhaps hoping to naturally inspire our faith and trust in God. In this way, his appeal would be able to land on fertile ground and take root.

Of course, our being asked to put our very human (and perhaps very fragile) trust in God is a big ask. Yet the psalmist doesn't shy away from making his appeal. He beseeches us to make a turn toward the intimate and the vulnerable through putting our trust in God as a first step.

At this point, it's as if the psalmist intuits that we'd be hard pressed to offer any resistance to the invitation to trust. This is where it gets real because this is where we are going to be asked to fully open our hearts to God. Once we do, it's going to send reverberations backward to change the resonance of each of the qualities, to color them with not just the strength one may find in a king charged with protecting his people, but all God's qualities will take on a dimension of love. In other words, these qualities will now grow out of and have their being and meaning grounded in love, as if they belong to a lover or a parent or an intimate friend.

Pour Out Your Hearts Before Him, for God Is Our Refuge.

The words of this half verse of instruction ask us to do something that is almost too much of an ask. However, if we've been working with the instructions up to this point and have been engaging a regular centering prayer praxis, we will arrive at this moment with a willingness to be vulnerable and to put our trust in God.

Our vulnerability and trust bear witness to our faith in and our love for God. It's clear from this verse that trust is the necessary ingredient to be able to embrace this instruction and invitation, to be able to pour out our hearts before God in the safety and nurturing embrace of the Divine, who is truly our refuge.

A question about how we pour out our hearts to God during centering prayer may arise. It's certainly a logical question to raise in light of this instruction. In answer, we first need to recall that centering prayer is not discursive prayer. We don't use words in centering prayer, but that does not mean that communication isn't taking place. Pouring out our hearts to God is a simple process that involves three uncomplicated steps.

Pouring Out Our Hearts

Step 1: Notice.

Become aware of what you're feeling in your heart in the moment. No need to label it, simply become aware of the feeling.

Step 2: Stay.

Stay in your heart with God, who is already there with you. Stay in the emotion or feeling without moving into its story. Stay with what shows up. Stay with God.

Step 3: Give over.

Give over to God. Let God do as God sees fit to do with what you're experiencing in your heart at the moment.

Instructions Drawn From the Psalm

• Pouring out our hearts to God is the opposite of shutting down our hearts, the opposite of suppressing or dismissing an emotion or feeling.

• The instructions of Psalm 62 acknowledge that we need to have trust in God to be able to pour out our hearts to God.

• The psalmist offers the perfect instruction around having trust in God: *Put your trust in him always.* In other words, let's never falter for God will never fail us.

• The psalmist describes God as *our refuge*, and reminds us not only of the safety we find in God, but also how God's safety creates a nurturing shelter for us: the ultimate safe space.

• Standing in the stream of our intimate trust in God, we pour out our hearts, releasing to the Holy Spirit each long-held emotion and feeling that we have been clinging to so tightly.

Reflect

• Describe a time when you've had your trust broken. How did it affect you?

_____

_____

_____

_____

_____

_____

_____

• What needs to be in place for you to trust another and feel safe?

_____

_____

_____

_____

_____

_____

_____

• What may prevent you from trusting God?

_____

_____

_____

_____

_____

_____

_____

_____

_____

_____

• How would it be to allow yourself to give over to the Holy Spirit whatever is getting in the way of your trusting God?

_____

_____

_____

_____

CENTERING PRAYER

1	**SIT AND CLOSE YOUR EYES** In a quiet and calm space, sit and get comfortable. Then close your eyes.
2	**SETTLE INTO YOUR BODY** Take a few deep breaths through your nose as you become aware of your body.
3	**NOTICE YOUR HEART SPACE** Move to the Holy Ground of your heart space. Notice emotions/feelings the Holy Spirit offers. As you're able, be present with the emotions/feelings.
4	**LET THE EMOTIONS/FEELINGS SUBSIDE AND RELEASE THEM** Allow the emotions/feelings to subside and resolve. Then offer them back to the Holy Spirit.
5	**RETURN TO YOUR WAITING** As you release and offer the emotions/feelings back to the Holy Spirit, return to your waiting.
6	**SLOWLY OPEN YOUR EYES** As your centering prayer session comes to a close, bring your awareness to your breath, then to the whole of your body. After a few breaths, slowly open your eyes.

23

ANOTHER CHECK-IN

AT THIS POINT IN the instructions, we can easily see that the over-all direction of movement within our centering prayer praxis is from the mind to the heart. Part and parcel to this movement is a shift from discursive thoughts and stories toward the realm of pure feeling and emotion.

As most of us habitually live in the world of the mind, we tend to think and communicate in thoughts and stories. Because of this, we often find ourselves almost exclusively interacting and processing our world and life from the mind. This can make moving into our hearts more difficult. The instructions contained in Psalm 62 are presented in such a way as to help us realize this fact naturally, and then offer guidance to help us discover and remain in the heart.

The most recent dynamic we have explored ends (verse 9) with an earnest invitation to enter more deeply into trust and vulnerability (necessary for entering the heart space) through a pouring out or emptying of our hearts to God. However, if we stay in our stories and thoughts (our minds), this pouring out of our hearts to God becomes more challenging. Remember that we're moving from discursive thoughts and stories toward pure feeling and emotion (from head to heart). The process outlined at the end of the last chapter presented a method or approach for the pouring out of our hearts (emotions/feelings) to God.

If you've never tried to move from thoughts and stories to the underlying feelings and emotions, the process may take some practice and getting used to. However, you can practice it outside of centering prayer at any point during the day. Simply become aware of a thought or story you're experiencing, then tap into the emotion or feeling associated with it while letting the storyline drop away. It's the emotion or feeling that is actually giving it life.

As you practice this process, it's important to remember that you don't need to do anything with the emotion or feeling. You don't even need to label it as a particular type of emotion or feeling. Just notice it without engaging it.

In working with this process, you'll discover something that you may not have considered. You'll discover that without the supply of "energy" from the feeling or emotion, the thought or story becomes gauzy and light, and it simply dissolves. We'll learn more about this in the upcoming dynamic. However, for now, it's enough to start to become aware of this fact experientially through practice.

Key Points

• Centering prayer is not a discursive form of prayer. Rather, it is a form of prayer that moves us from the mind into the heart, where emotions and feelings are the currency of communication instead of words, thoughts, and stories.

• Developing the skill to experience our emotions and feelings without the words, thoughts, and stories that they fuel takes practice. This practice does not have to be done solely during centering prayer.

Reflection

• Describe where in your body that you notice pure emotions or feelings, without their accompanying thoughts.

_____

_____

_____

_____

_____

CENTERING PRAYER

1	**SIT AND CLOSE YOUR EYES** In a quiet and calm space, sit and get comfortable. Then close your eyes.
2	**SETTLE INTO YOUR BODY** Take a few deep breaths through your nose as you become aware of your body.
3	**REST IN YOUR HEART SPACE** Gently move your awareness to your heart space. Become aware of how your waiting feels.
4	**NOTICE AND OFFER YOUR THOUGHTS** As you notice thoughts that the Holy Spirit brings into your awareness, release and offer them back to the Holy Spirit. Then return to your Holy Ground.
5	**EXPLORE** Once again in the Holy Ground of your heart, be present to how it is different this time. Notice all that comes into your awareness.
6	**SLOWLY OPEN YOUR EYES** As your centering prayer session comes to a close, bring your awareness to your breath, then to the whole of your body. After a few breaths, slowly open your eyes.

24

THOSE OF HIGH DEGREE ARE BUT A FLEETING BREATH...

AT THIS POINT IN the psalm (verse 10), we find ourselves being introduced to the next dynamic of centering prayer with the somewhat unsettling words (yet wise counsel): *Those of high degree are but a fleeting breath, even those of low estate cannot be trusted.* As you may have suspected, this dynamic focuses again on the thoughts that inhabit our minds.

Since we live so much of our lives in our minds, we often become desensitized to how much weight we give our thoughts and how attached we become to them as they fill and swirl around our minds. In fact, many of us have placed so much trust in our thoughts that we have let them govern our lives, often leading us to orient ourselves and our hearts toward these very same thoughts instead of toward God.

As we know, one of the benefits of a centering prayer praxis is that it helps us to refocus our hearts toward God. This reorienting of our lives toward God may be an on-going process for many of us, one that is filled with eye-opening discoveries about how much power we have given to our thoughts and, in many cases, to their unsubstantiated lies that we take as truth about ourselves, the world, and even God.

The instructions that we find in this particular dynamic help us to gain experiential understanding of the nature of our thoughts, and, in particular, those that keep us far from God.

High Degree

The first half of verse 10 focuses on thoughts of high degree and how they are "a fleeting breath." It helps to see these high thoughts as reflections of how we view ourselves and our actions as being superlative. Let's look at a few examples to get a more concrete idea of the types of thoughts that would fall into this category.

Most thoughts of "high degree" cause us to feel like we are in a category above the general population. For example, we may think of ourselves as so spiritual that we have all the answers about God or that we don't need practices like centering prayer. Another example would be acting in prideful ways about our centering prayer praxis. That may look like viewing ourselves as better than another because we never miss a praxis period while others do. The bottom line is that thoughts of "high degree" make us feel self-righteous in comparison to others and their actions (or lack thereof).

These particular thoughts are said to be a "fleeting breath." This imagery astutely calls out the lack of importance of these thoughts. In reality, like a fleeting breath, these thoughts have no weight, and they effect or bring about nothing of substance or worth.

If you recall, in verse 8, the psalmist writes about how we get our true honor or worth from the "weightiness" of God. These thoughts of "high degree" are, in fact, the polar opposite and as weighty as a fleeting breath. Though we may take pride in ourselves as a result of thinking them, they have no worth and add nothing to what is real about ourselves, which we derive directly through our relationship with God.

Low Estate

If we turn to the second half of verse 10, we observe that the psalmist focuses on the opposite end of the spectrum, bringing our attention to thoughts of "low estate." These thoughts have no value for us as they "cannot be trusted."

Thoughts associated with low self-esteem serve as a good example of "low-estate" thoughts. These can range from thinking we are not good enough, not smart enough, or not worthy of love, to name just a few. Any thought that might give us permission to beat ourself up for an action, inaction, or feeling a certain way qualifies as a "low-estate" thought.

The take-away is they cannot be trusted. The single directive of this type of thought is to take us down a path of misery and suffering. The message of low-estate thoughts is false despite that it may feel true or accurate. If we trust these thoughts and believe that they offer an accurate assessment of who we are, then we move out of alignment with God. In the end, the thoughts win and we suffer.

An Exercise in Awareness

As a way to start to become aware of how invasive and influential these two categories of thought are in our lives, let's commit to take notice when they show up in the mind. This may take some practice. However, when we do become aware of one of these thoughts or trains of thought, we can pause what we're doing (if it is safe to do so), and notice what's happening in the body at that moment. Also, we can notice if the thought lives in a particular area of the body.

This can be a revealing activity. It's good to remember that we will get the most out of it when we don't approach it as a vigilante on the hunt for "criminal" thoughts. Instead, let's approach this exercise from the space of curiosity. It's simply about becoming aware of how these kinds of thoughts show up in the mind as well as how they inhabit the body or the types of sensations they create in the body.

Instructions Drawn From the Psalm

• Two particularly destabilizing types of thoughts that we may experience and become more aware of during centering prayer are those of "high degree" and those of "low estate."

• High-degree thoughts include those that contribute to self-aggrandizement. Low-estate thoughts are just the opposite and initiate or reinforce low self-esteem.

Reflection

• After gaining experiential awareness of how these types of thoughts show up in your mind and body, reflect on what stands out for you. How do these thoughts personally affect your relationships with others and with God?

_____

_____

_____

_____

_____

CENTERING PRAYER

1 **SIT AND CLOSE YOUR EYES**
In a quiet and calm space, sit and get comfortable. Then close your eyes.

2 **SETTLE INTO YOUR BODY**
Take a few deep breaths through your nose as you become aware of your body.

3 **REST IN YOUR HEART SPACE**
Gently move your awareness to your heart space. Become aware of how your waiting feels.

4 **NOTICE AND OFFER YOUR THOUGHTS**
As you notice thoughts that the Holy Spirit brings into your awareness, release and offer them back to the Holy Spirit. Then return to your Holy Ground.

5 **EXPLORE**
Once again in the Holy Ground of your heart, be present to how it is different this time. Notice all that comes into your awareness.

6 **SLOWLY OPEN YOUR EYES**
As your centering prayer session comes to a close, bring your awareness to your breath, then to the whole of your body. After a few breaths, slowly open your eyes.

25

⌒⌒⌒

ON THE SCALES,
THEY ARE LIGHTER
THAN A BREATH...

As WE STUDY VERSE 11 to discern its instruction, we notice that
the imagery of breath from the previous verse reappears. The
psalmist skillfully develops and furthers the spirit of the instruction introduced in verse 10 through this image of breath: *On the
scales, they are lighter than a breath, all of them together.*

He presents us with the scene of a scale with all the thoughts
of high degree and low estate on one side, and a single breath
on the other side. In this scene, we observe that the collective
weight of these thoughts doesn't begin to match that of a single
breath. Such a simple yet dramatic image delivers a powerful
impression and conveys an important instruction.

In English, the sentence *That argument carries no weight*
gets to the heart of what this verse is saying about these types

of thoughts. They carry no weight. Their arguments, what they are trying to convince us of, not only aren't valid, but they are insignificant and unimportant. They essentially have no weight. Further to that, we should not give them weight; we should not become attached to them.

To underscore the significance of weight to convey the idea of worth, let's recall that in verse 8, our weightiness—our significance and worth—comes from God. Therefore, it only stands to reason that thoughts like these "high-degree" and "low-estate" thoughts are surely insignificant and worthless and have no truth because they have no weight, which corresponds to God-given worth.

Thoughts Considered

Here's one final note to consider in regard to thoughts of any sort. While they have no physical qualities and are, as such, lighter than a breath, they do have the power (if we engage them and give them weight) to infect and affect many aspects of our life, particularly if left unexamined.

This point is worth lingering over and pondering. Consider how thought underpins our actions. Thought determines which actions we take. Thought colors the lens we use to judge our actions and ourselves. Thought can torment us, delude us, or support us. Thought influences how we engage with the world and with ourselves. Given all of this, thought is actually rather amazing. Of course, as we'll explore in the next chapter, something underpins our thoughts to give them life and power. But for now, take a few moments to reflect on your thoughts and how they infect and affect aspects of your life.

Connection to Centering Prayer

How does all of this relate to centering prayer? It draws our attention to the important role that each non-silent moment of thought noise plays in our centering prayer. These are not wasted moments in our centering prayer, though initially we may believe them to be or even get frustrated by them. On the contrary, when the Holy Spirit brings these thoughts into our awareness, we can recall these instructions and note these thoughts for what they are. In doing so, we will be able more easily to offer them back to the Holy Spirit.

In essence, our offering them to the Holy Spirit leads to our releasing them to the Holy Spirit, who will take them and dissolve them. If we're present enough, we can even feel the sensation of the Holy Spirit's action. It may be quite subtle, but it *is* registered in our bodies.

Handing Over

It's important to understand that this action of handing over to the Holy Spirit is not the same as suppressing the thoughts. Handing over our thoughts to the Holy Spirit is healthy and moves us into deeper trust and relationship with God. Suppressing our thoughts, on the other hand, is a type of maladaptive coping strategy with which we push our thoughts outside our awareness. We do this consciously, often thinking it wise or our only option to be able to function or cope with our reality.

Instructions Drawn From the Psalm

• Although thoughts have no physical qualities or physical weight, they often infect and affect many aspects of our life. This is particularly the case if we don't spend time examining our thoughts.

• In centering prayer, we hand over our thoughts to the Holy Spirit. We release them. We do not suppress them.

• Spending time outside of centering prayer to better understand the role thoughts play in our life, as well as which thoughts we give more power, will help bring this instruction to life.

•The value of this instruction lies in how it empowers us to hand over and release our thoughts to the Holy Spirit; it helps us to break our attachment to our thoughts.

Reflection

• Reflect on how your thoughts influence your relationships. Then describe how they impact one of those relationships.

_____

_____

_____

_____

_____

_____

_____

_____

• Notice how your thoughts impact your relationship with God. How does that show up for you?

_____

_____

_____

_____

_____

_____

_____

_____

CENTERING PRAYER

1

SIT AND CLOSE YOUR EYES
In a quiet and calm space, sit either on the floor, on a cushion, or in a chair. Get comfortable. Close your eyes.

2

SETTLE INTO YOUR BODY
Take a few deep breaths through your nose. Allow yourself to become aware of your body as you say to yourself "For God alone my soul in silence waits."

3

BREATHE INTO YOUR HEART SPACE
Shift your awareness to your breath. Let your breath be the vehicle that moves your awareness into your heart space.

4

REST IN YOUR HEART SPACE
Allow your awareness to expand slightly from your heart space until you notice subtle sensations like butterflies in your stomach. This is your Holy Ground. Rest here in waiting.

5

NOTICE AND OFFER YOUR THOUGHTS
As you notice thoughts that the Holy Spirit brings into your awareness, release and offer them back to the Holy Spirit. Then return to your Holy Ground and waiting.

6

SLOWLY OPEN YOUR EYES
As your centering prayer session comes to a close, bring your awareness to your breath, then to the whole of your body. After a few breaths, slowly open your eyes.

26

PUT NO TRUST IN EXTORTION...

WITH THE TWO PREVIOUS verses, the psalmist has presented us with a mini-opus on thoughts that is both provocative and instructive. Now, he concludes this dynamic of centering prayer with *Put no trust in extortion; in robbery take no empty pride; though wealth increase, set not your heart upon it.*

Let's unpack three of this verse's key phrases: *extortion, robbery*, and *increase of wealth*. Each of these can stand on its own; however, we're going to approach them in relationship to each other. The first two will lead to the third. In other words, through extortion and robbery, our wealth will increase. Of course, we're being counseled to put no trust in extortion, take no empty pride in robbery, and not to desire the wealth that arrives through extortion and robbery. Good counsel for sure, but how does it apply to centering prayer?

Getting Clear About the False Self's Mission

Before answering the question above, let's take a moment to introduce a necessary topic to the conversation: the false self. Most of us have a general idea or working definition of terms like *ego* and *false self*. In brief, *ego* is a term used to name that part in each of us that we most often identify with. It's that sense of *I* that we possess. The ego certainly plays an essential role in our daily lives, getting us safely through each moment. However, the ego is prone to develop an aspect that wants to take control in maladaptive and unhealthy ways. When that happens, we can refer to that corrupted part of the ego as the false self.

The kicker is that we all have a false self, and at the end of the day, our false self wants us to itself. It wants to be the god of our lives. Our false self doesn't want us to transform our lives through centering prayer; it doesn't want us to orient our hearts to God; it doesn't want us to secure and deepen a relationship with God. These actions threaten the autonomy that the false self craves, making it desperate to shore up control of our life and our world if it feels its power slipping away.

When threatened in these ways, the false self can resort to subtle but highly effective tactics to bring us back in line, causing us to fail at centering prayer. At this point, we acknowledge that if our centering prayer fails, then actions are set in motion that can destabilize our relationship with God while securing the false self's place once again as lord and master over us.

Let's not underestimate the power of the false self's plots as they're outlined in this verse. At first glance, the tactics spoken about may all seem like simple games on the part of the false self–easily spotted and disrupted. However, if we fall into that mindset, then we've already started down the path that leads to a win for the false self.

Now, let's unpack the three key phrases mentioned above, working from the last to the first.

Increase of Wealth

Wealth can be likened to a feeling of accomplishment or success. We know how it feels when we have lots of money in the bank. Not only do we feel successful, but we also start to lose sight of what is important, of what life is really about. Why does this happen? Because we become attached to the feeling associated with excess money (a.k.a. wealth).

Such an attachment starts to change our relationship to life itself. It shifts our focus from our relationship with God to our desire to gain more wealth. This reorients our heart, driving us to make ourselves into the god and controller of our destiny and our world. It puts us on a slippery slope, potentially leading us to make decisions that move us out of alignment with God, and all in the name of gaining more wealth.

Given that scenario, let's also read the increase of wealth called out in this verse as a stockpiling of all the centering prayer sessions that leave us feeling accomplished and like we had a "good" centering prayer experience.

When we let the false self qualify our centering prayer experiences (e.g., *good* as opposed to *bad*), then we may start to get attached to the "good" experiences and start to desire a "good" outcome each time we enter into centering prayer. If we start to entertain these desires, we're giving over to the false self.

We may even find the false self trying to manipulate and control a session to give us the satisfaction of having had a "good" centering prayer experience. In short, "good" or "successful" centering prayer experiences become a sort of currency that the false self wants to stockpile. We let the false self turn them into "wealth." Setting our hearts on this kind of "wealth" is what the psalmist explicitly cautions against in this instruction.

To be clear, we are not being told that we will never have centering prayer experiences that will feel good, because we will. However, we're being cautioned against desiring them, expecting them, attaching our heart to them, and using them as a measurement of the quality of our praxis. In other words and in those of the psalmist, we are instructed to *set not your heart upon it.* More precisely, we should not fall into the use of dualistic labels like *good* or *bad* to determine the value, worth, and wealth of any centering prayer session. Each is valuable. Each has its own profound and rich worth because each session heals and restores our intimate and subjective relationship with God.

Now, let's look at the tactics that will most likely lead to the temptation of setting our heart on such "increased wealth."

Robbery and Pride

When we deprive centering prayer of its inherent validity and worth, regardless of what happens in any of our centering prayer sessions, then the false self has succeeded in robbing us of the life-changing range of experiences that lead to and sustain a vibrant and healing relationship with God. When the false self robs us, it is actually stealing our faith and trust in God. That is serious and can't be overstated.

One sign that points toward this is an awareness of attachment (or even addiction) to feelings of pride that come about as a result of our validation of only the "good" or "noteworthy" experiences of centering prayer.

This "empty pride" fuels the false self, giving it power and strength to destabilize our centering prayer praxis, while at the same time undermining our relationship with God.

The solution to this scenario, we are told, is to disregard this sense of pride as it is empty and unjustified. If we follow this instruction, we can disempower the false self when it engages in such robbery and reorient the heart toward God, allowing for a restoration of relationship with the Divine that the false self had eroded.

Extortion

Extortion is the act of gaining something unfairly. For our purposes, the false self can also act as an extortionist resorting to crafty ingenuity, compelling arguments, and some convincing mental gymnastics to make us feel self-satisfied, and to gain or maintain control. In short, the false self wants to be our god and reign supreme in our world.

Let's recall that to avoid this type of extortion, we must not fall prey to the false self's scheming. We must not trust the false self's brilliant and compelling arguments used to convince us of the necessity for the "wealth" that comes about from amassing the satisfying feelings of success and accomplishment which arise from judging our centering prayer.

Working With the Plan of Action

The instruction presented in this verse alerts us to three subtle tactics that the false self may take to safeguard its control over us. Along with these tactics, the psalmist gives us specific ways to counter them, all which have to do with misplaced trust and attachment. To sum them up, we don't trust or become attached to or set our hearts on any of these tactics and their seductions. To bring this important instruction to life in our centering prayer and beyond, we can hone and implement a three-fold action plan or skill set based on awareness, release, and orientation.

Our first action needs to focus on initiating and maintaining an internal awareness that acknowledges any of these false-self-driven thoughts and feelings, which can often be subtle. This initial step is critical because we can do nothing about the tactics if we don't realize they're taking place.

Next, we avoid listening to or following these false-self-driven thoughts and feelings. As we become aware of the false self's tactics, we can easily fall under their spell and give ourselves over to believing them. In short, we stand on the precipice of temptation as we become aware of these thoughts; therefore, let's stay cognizant of that potential and, instead of giving over to them, we launch into the third part of our plan of action. We orient or turn our awareness to God.

As we turn toward God, we set our hearts on God and release any attachment to the tactics and any of the associated thoughts or feelings. This action also reinforces our commitment against suppressing these types of thoughts and feelings. The danger of suppression, as we've pointed out earlier, is that at some point the suppressed thoughts will resurface, and usually with more energy than they originally had.

The action within centering prayer that helps us set our heart on God is the act of consciously handing over our thoughts. We offer them or hand them over to the Holy Spirit, releasing them and thereby no longer fueling them with our focus.

Outside of Centering Prayer

It's valuable for us also to understand that these tactics on the part of the false self often take place outside of centering prayer, too. Regardless of when the false self invades with these particular thoughts and feelings, the effect will still lead to a destabilization of our centering prayer praxis and eventually our relationship with God and others.

Love and Compassion

Throughout this dynamic of centering prayer, it's important for us to make a distinction between pointing out the actions of the false self and demonizing or scapegoating the false self.

While it is true that the actions and tactics of the false self are not healthy and are dysfunctional, it is also true that the false self's actions arise from a maladaptive coping strategy employed to help us deal with fear and unhealed wounds.

At the end of the day, the false self is part of our ego, which is a part of each of us, and which God created. We need to hold the false self in compassion and love, while also seeing it clearly for what it is. In this way, we remain in alignment and relationship with God and don't fall prey to the very same fear that controls the false self.

Instructions Drawn From the Psalm

• Stay aware of the false self. It can become the satan of centering prayer, causing us to judge our experiences, robbing and extorting us of our faith, trust, and relationship with God.

• The false self will use our centering prayer to anoint itself with "power" and "wealth." When this happens, the false self effectively crowns itself as god within the realm of our centering prayer, while gaining control of our lives.

• Do not underestimate the draw of the "wealth" that the false self presents us through our centering prayer.

• When we heed the guidance of the instruction and put no trust in the games of the false self, we disempower it and remain firm, with our heart centered on God.

• It is important not to demonize or scape goat the false self. We need to see it for what it is while also holding it in love and compassion.

Reflection

• Review the information about guilt, shame, and frustration in Chapter 1. Describe how these compare to the false self's tactics described in this chapter.

_____

_____

_____

_____

_____

_____

_____

_____

• Reflect on your centering prayer experiences in relation to the psalmist's description of the false self's tactics. How do they show up for you?

_____

_____

_____

_____

• When do you most often fall prey to the tactics of the false self?

_____

_____

_____

_____

_____

_____

_____

• Describe your relationship with the false self.

_____

_____

_____

_____

• What can you do to develop compassion and love for the false self, if it is lacking?

_____

_____

_____

CENTERING PRAYER

1

SIT, CLOSE YOUR EYES, AND SETTLE
In a quiet and calm space, sit and get comfortable.
Then close your eyes as you settle into your body.

2

REPEAT THE PSALM'S TWENTY-FIFTH/TWENTY-SIXTH LINES
Recall the twenty-fifth and twenty-sixth lines of Psalm
62: *God has spoken once....* Slowly say each word. Linger
on those words that you feel drawn to linger on.

3

SURRENDER TO GOD
Notice how surrendered to God you are. Become
aware of how it is showing up in your body.

4

REST IN YOUR HEART SPACE
Gently move your awareness to your heart space.
Notice and explore your experience of surrender to
God while in your heart space.

5

LET THE EMOTIONS/FEELINGS SUBSIDE AND RELEASE THEM
Allow any emotions/feelings to subside and resolve.
Then offer them back to the Holy Spirit. Return to
your waiting.

6

SLOWLY OPEN YOUR EYES
As your centering prayer session comes to a close,
bring your awareness to your breath, then to the whole
of your body. After a few breaths, slowly open your
eyes.

27

❦

God Has Spoken Once, Twice I Have Heard It...

We now come face to face with the final dynamic of centering prayer and the final set of instructions presented to us through Psalm 62. Let's begin by looking at the entire verse.

God has spoken once, twice have I heard it,
that power belongs to God.

Cryptic for Good Reason

To be honest, the opening words that introduce us to this final dynamic are rather cryptic. They sound a bit like a Zen koan, leaving us with the feeling that their meaning is just out of reach and ever-so-slightly beyond our understanding.

To be fair, those hearing this verse in the time it was written would have been able to understand the expression with little difficulty. However, to our modern ears, the ancient expression causes the verse to open in a puzzling way, yet actually adds a wonderful layer of meaning for us.

It serves, in part, as a final reminder that our relationship with God is always going to surpass our understanding. It's simply the nature of God and God's love for us. This supernatural relationship is always ever fresh, ever expanding, and eternally deepening.

This is the knowledge that the curiosity-provoking, head-scratching words of this half verse call us always to re-member. God's love for us is exciting. It's always asking us to grow into the eternally new horizons of love that we are des-tined for in Christ. It may be a good idea to pause and spend a little time reflecting on the previous sentences.

On Another Level

Another level of guidance that this half verse provides us is slightly more literal. It's a reminder that as God speaks, we would do well to hear it twice. More precisely, we need to hear it resonating in two different places within us: the heart and the mind.

In the silence of centering prayer, when we are within the space of our hearts, God speaks, and we hear once. Hearing God while in this heart space is different than hearing God outside of it. Within our hearts, God approaches us beyond the discursiveness of words, and it is here that we receive what God "speaks" to us. We don't act on it. We allow it to fill our heart space with the fullness of God's love, transforming us and healing our wounds.

As we move back into the world of words and discursive thoughts, back into the experience of our minds, we hear again ("twice") what God has "spoken" in our heart space. This time, however, words and thoughts begin to form in the mind to articulate what God "spoke" while we were in our centering prayer and in the space of our hearts. Through these newly formed words and thoughts, we may be left with a clear idea about how we can respond in our daily life to what we heard God "speak" to us, not only once, but twice.

Surrendering to God

Now, let's turn our attention to the second part of this verse: *that power belongs to God.* It points us toward how we need to orient our hearts. It speaks to the fact that power does not belong to us nor to our thoughts. Power is God's. In short, we are not God, and our thoughts are not God. As we continue to show up for centering prayer, we will get this in an experiential and intimate way.

Moving more deeply into this awareness, and in connection with hearing in the heart first, and then in the mind, we are led toward an understanding that the heart naturally orients toward God. However, wounding in our heart space can affect its natural orientation, which then leads to the mind swirling out of its natural orientation, too. In such cases, as we move from our wounded heart space back into our minds, we may find that so much is vying for godship that we get distracted and overwhelmed, and often end up orienting our minds toward all manner of things that we make into gods and that, in turn, influence or dictate our actions. When this happens, we experience discord or dissonance between head and heart. We move out of alignment with God.

This instruction, when played out in full, shines light on and connects our rightly aligned actions in the world with the natural orientation of our hearts. As we properly orient our hearts, our physical actions flow from that genesis point where God speaks them to us in our hearts, and then their essence gets articulated in our rightly oriented minds, leading us to actualize them in the world of our day-to-day life. Fundamentally, this all begins when we surrender to our God instead of to our gods.

Of course, how we surrender to our God instead of our gods will look different for each of us. As the psalmist reminds us, during centering prayer, God will speak into our hearts, and we will witness (hear) it spoken a second time in our minds. From that place of informed mind, we'll understand what surrendering to our God looks like. Experience will bring its own clarity.

Instructions Drawn From the Psalm

• God and our relationship with God is ever fresh, ever deepening, and ever expanding.

• God "speaks" to us in our hearts. We hear it there once, and then hear it a second time as it gets translated into words in our minds, finally leading to actions in our bodies.

• God's power is not our power. We are not God. We orient our hearts to God in surrender to overcome the gods in our life.

Reflection

• Reflect on the gods in your life that demand your surrender. Why does each hold power over you?

_____

_____

_____

_____

CENTERING PRAYER

1	**SIT, CLOSE YOUR EYES, AND SETTLE** In a quiet and calm space, sit and get comfortable. Then close your eyes as you settle into your body.
2	**REPEAT THE FINAL TWO LINES OF THE PSALM** Recall final two lines of Psalm 62: *Steadfast love is yours....* Slowly say each word. Linger on those words that you feel drawn to linger on.
3	**NOTICE SENSATIONS IN YOUR BODY** Become aware of the idea of steadfast love. Notice how your body responds.
4	**REST IN YOUR HEART SPACE** Gently move your awareness to your heart space. Notice and explore your experience of the steadfast love of God while in your heart space.
5	**LET THE EMOTIONS/FEELINGS SUBSIDE AND RELEASE THEM** Allow any emotions/feelings to subside and resolve. Then offer them back to the Holy Spirit. Return to your Holy Ground and notice.
6	**SLOWLY OPEN YOUR EYES** As your centering prayer session comes to a close, bring your awareness to your breath, then to the whole of your body. After a few breaths, slowly open your eyes.

28

STEADFAST LOVE IS
YOURS, O LORD...

IF EVER THERE WERE words written that could stir us to willingly and completely give ourselves over to intimacy and love for God, surely those that the psalmist leaves us with in his parting verse would qualify.

Through his evocative, almost haunting words, he leaves us with one final instruction as both reminder and invitation: *Steadfast love is yours, O Lord, for you repay everyone according to his deeds.*

Steadfast Love

We're told over and over again in Holy Scripture that God is love. A good question to ask is *How often does that message have to be repeated before we get it as reality and not just as theory?*

The simple answer, based on the textual evidence we have from the pages of the Bible, is *a lot*. It seems most of us are almost hardwired to disbelieve the statements about God being love. If on a good day, we do start to believe it, at least theoretically, it often doesn't last. Many of us become overwhelmed again all too quickly by our own brokenness, and we're thrown right back into disbelief. Sin does its part, too. As we move out of harmony with God, we move into that realm of disbelief about God being love and maybe even about God's very existence.

A good antidote to all of this is to show up for centering prayer.

In support of our commitment to centering prayer, the instructions provided by Psalm 62 have devoted lots of real estate to describe the qualities of God's love. Recall words like *safety*, *refuge*, *stronghold*. Each of these words helps us to recognize that God's love nurtures and heals. Each word builds into a crescendo that leads to a continual opening of our minds and hearts, making us ready not just to hear but to receive this final verse and Psalm 62's last description of God's love: its steadfast nature.

Reflect on the role that knowledge plays in moving us into the type of trust necessary for us to be open to a relationship with God that is as vulnerable, tender, and intimate as it is dynamic, vibrant, and ever deepening. Ponder how essential it is for us to know that God's love is steadfast. Let this quality of God's love reverberate throughout your body as you receive it as an essential part of this final instruction.

With the Eye of a Mystic

For the final half verse, using the lens or eye of a Christian mystic will make clear the psalmist's instruction. In other words, our interpretation will be grounded in unity and wholeness, harmonizing the entire verse through the only true harmonizer: love. God does repay us according to our deeds with the only thing God has or is...and that is love, a love that is freely and steadfastly (continuously) given.

Repay...According to His Deeds

This idea of God repaying everyone may catch us slightly off-guard. It's a provocative statement that can intrigue the reader, but it also serves to energize this particular instruction. Suggesting that God repays us also suggests that the God who needs nothing has actually borrowed from us. Let's stay in the vision of a mystic as we unpack what that means.

The whole borrow-and-repay dynamic can be distilled down to the idea of an exchange: a giving or handing over that merits a return or a giving back. It may also help us to keep in mind the idea of a flow between two parties to maintain a certain type of continual and unobstructed reciprocity in relationship.

Now, let's recall how we release or hand over our deeds and actions that the Holy Spirit calls into our mind during centering prayer. We have often made these deeds and actions, as well as any accompanying thoughts, into gods and masters of our lives, giving them our power and allowing them to control and inflict us with hurt and wounds. They infect our love and affect how we offer and receive love. With that understanding, as we give over these deeds, actions, and thoughts to the Holy Spirit, we use our vulnerable and often broken love as the energetic or flow that carries them into the arms of the Holy Spirit.

Then God receives our love that we have given, which is infused with, for example, hate or hurt or brokenness or whatever our lived experience has inflicted upon us through deed or action.

As God receives this from us through the Holy Spirit, God returns or pays us back with pure, holy, healing love. This rarefied love overflows with divine compassion and nurturing and understanding in the measure required to heal the pain, wound, and hurt, all born out of our deeds and actions and that live in our being. It is in this sense that God repays everyone *according to his deeds.*

Some of our deeds cause us more pain and more hurt than others. We need not fear because in the economy of God's love, the more our hurt, the more of God's full, overflowing, and steadfast love we receive.

Promise and Invitation

If we humbly come to centering prayer in faith and trust, expecting to meet God in our heart, then our centering prayer experience will become a testament to the value of these instructions.

This beautiful, liberating, and poignant half verse that ends our psalm of instructions is, in essence, a gentle promise and a heart-felt invitation beckoning us to fall in love with and remain in the reality that is the ever-caring, steadfast love of God.

Instructions Drawn From the Psalm

• Spend time each day reflecting on the many qualities that imbue God's love, including its steadfastness.

• Until we gain experience with these instructions, we may need to use the eye of the Christian mystic to be present to their nuance and layers of meaning.

• God always repays us with pure and nurturing love.

• We will do well to hear the centering prayer instructions of Psalm 62 as promise and invitation.

Reflect

• Reflect on the qualities of God's love that you've experienced in your life. Describe each of those qualities or facets.

_____

_____

_____

_____

_____

_____

_____

_____

• Explore the idea of flow as in the *flow of communication.* How does belief in punishment or retribution disrupt it?

_____

_____

_____

_____

• How have you seen this play out in your relationship with others and with God?

_____

_____

_____

_____

_____

_____

_____

_____

• The invitation found in the last verse of Psalm 62 is, in essence, a call to remain in the steadfast love of God. How does this invitation land with you? Describe how it feels as you receive it in your heart.

_____

_____

_____

_____

CENTERING PRAYER

1 | **SIT, CLOSE YOUR EYES, AND SETTLE**
In a quiet and calm space, sit and get comfortable. Then close your eyes as you settle into your body.

2 | **REPEAT THE FINAL TWO LINES OF THE PSALM**
Recall final two lines of Psalm 62: *Steadfast love is yours....* Slowly say each word. Linger on those words that you feel drawn to linger on.

3 | **SENSE THE INVITATION FROM GOD**
Become aware of God's invitation. Notice how your body responds.

4 | **REST IN YOUR HEART SPACE**
Gently move your awareness to your heart space. Notice your experience of receiving invitation from God while in your heart space.

5 | **LET THE EMOTIONS/FEELINGS SUBSIDE AND RELEASE THEM**
Allow any emotions/feelings to subside and resolve. Then offer them back to the Holy Spirit. Return to God.

6 | **SLOWLY OPEN YOUR EYES**
As your centering prayer session comes to a close, bring your awareness to your breath, then to the whole of your body. After a few breaths, slowly open your eyes.

EPILOGUE

IN THE GENTLE BREEZE

CENTERING PRAYER HOLDS SUCH promise for the world, and in turn, for each of us. On some level, we've all been wounded, and our relationship with God has suffered. Therein lies the promise and potential of centering prayer. It offers each of us healing and restoration of our subjective relationship with God. What could be more worthwhile than that?

As a way to pay homage to Psalm 62 with its wisdom and instructions for centering prayer, let's spend some time with the following experience of the imagination. Let it inform and fuel our commitment to a lifelong praxis of centering prayer and an ever-fresh, ever-deepening relationship with God as we find ourselves again walking in the gentle breeze of Eden.

To Prepare

Begin by sitting in a comfortable and quiet place. As you slowly read the following words, allow them to flow into your imagination. Give it permission to create a scene that comes to life and saturates your senses. Let whatever unfolds find a home deep in the cells of your body, finally coming to rest in the intimate space of your heart.

In the Gentle Breeze

As you settle into your interior landscape, you find yourself in a realm that seems deprived and harsh. Maybe it's dry and desert-like or barren and lonely. Whatever the landscape is, invite your imagination to bring it more clearly into view.

As this realm makes itself known, spend time using all of your senses to explore what shows up.

While becoming familiar with the landscape, something in the distance catches your eye. As you look in that direction, you notice that a light shimmers on the horizon. It's like a beacon. The more you observe it, the more you feel a longing for it. You find yourself allowing that longing to move you gently through the landscape and toward that shimmering light in the distance.

As you move closer to the beacon, you become aware of feelings of loneliness and disconnectedness. A host of voices speak from within you. They are the voices born out of years of pain and wounding. It's as if this present world, the one that you currently inhabit, is now populated with memories and events, deeds, actions, and thoughts that coalesce into a barrier between you and something better, something you sense but can't quite identify.

You remain present to all that you're experiencing and become aware that your forward movement is slowing down, finally coming to a still point at the foot of the beacon.

As you look up, your gaze becomes fixed on several luminous beings. You notice that what you're taking in with your eyes can also be felt as sensations in your body. These luminous beings, these cherubim, wield what appear to be large swords of fire. These swords reflect the light of a sun high overhead. It's this reflected light that has been reaching into the distance of your world and calling for your attention.

As your gaze lowers to eye level, you notice a portal or gate upon which the cherubim stand. You can actually see on all sides of the gate what lies beyond it: a landscape utterly different from the one you inhabit now. The vegetation is rich and colorful and lush; the trees are in bloom with a multitude of flowers. Their petals gently fall and carpet the ground with softness. The very air itself shimmers, rarefied and alive.

Now, you notice some type of energy field or forcefield that separates your world from that which is on the other side of the gate.

As you continue to study it and take in the scene before you with all your senses, you slowly become aware of events flowing through your mind, flowing up from your heart. These events and images and words are new and different and yet somehow feel familiar, like fragments of memories that ebb and flow, elusive and just out of reach. You sense that they're memories of a time before you were separated from the realm that lies on the other side of the gate.

Your awareness is drawn inward to an unmistakable longing as it fills your heart. It's a longing to be on the other side of the energy field.

At this moment, you become aware of how the memories start to become clearer and take shape in your mind's eye: experiences of joy and easeful living. At the same time, you notice that a love is growing in your heart to the point of feeling as if it's going to burst forth from your body.

You try to tamp the sensation down as you begin to feel it turn your world upside down.

Suddenly the love bursts forth uncontrollably from your heart. Its bright and beautiful light connects with the light of the cherubim's swords.

At that precise moment, the forcefield dissipates, and the beauty and sweetness of the landscape that was once on the other side of that forcefield floods outward, expanding and transforming your landscape into Paradise.

The temperature shifts as a cool, welcoming breeze flows over the land. You feel it on your face, against your skin.

You look toward the cherubim, but they've disappeared.

As you sweep your eyes over the newly transformed landscape, you notice that a sweet aroma fills the air. At the same time, the soft warmth of some effusive light fills your heart as it washes over you.

In this moment, you experience that your heart is full of love. Yet, despite all the beauty of this place, one thing acutely stands out: a sense of longing in your heart.

It's like a silence that pulses with a knowing, a sense that someone whom you've not seen or been in the presence of in a very long time is arriving. Your anticipation grows as love starts to rise from your heart.

A moment more, and you hear a voice call your name. Your love responds by leaping forward toward the voice.

Another moment and your eyes behold an image that is both ancient and new. Your Lord, your friend, your lover approaches; and you're overcome with wave after wave of welcoming love.

Now, the Lord is beside you.

As you turn to face each other, you hear the Lord say....

Only you can write the ending of this experience. Only you can know what the Lord says to you as you find yourself once again in the Eden of your heart.

One Final Note

We've all cast ourselves out of Eden, out of the homeland of our hearts; and we've all placed cherubim at the gates to guard its entrance from all who might enter, including ourselves.

KEVIN SHARPE

However, each one of us can walk back into that garden that is our original home. Through centering prayer we can experience our return to Eden and to our easy walk with God in the evening's gentle breeze.

Join the Conversation

www.Facebook.com/groups/CenteringPrayer62